The Hidden Money Manual

Find Cash to Pay Your Bills Now

Gerry Marrs

Gerry Marrs Publications

First Edition

Published by
Gerry Marrs Publications
https://www.gerrymarrspublications.com

Disclaimer

This book is intended for informational and educational purposes only. The author is not a licensed financial advisor, accountant, or attorney. The material provided in this manual reflects the author's personal opinions and experiences and is not to be construed as professional financial, tax, or legal advice. Readers should consult with qualified professionals before making any financial decisions. The publisher and author disclaim any liability, loss, or risk incurred as a consequence, directly or indirectly, of the use or application of any of the contents of this book.

The inclusion of any websites, services, or external references does not constitute an endorsement by the author or publisher. These are provided for convenience and illustrative purposes only.

BISAC Subject Headings:

- BUS050000 — Business & Economics / Personal Finance / Money Management

- BUS001010 — Business & Economics / Budgeting

- BUS027000 — Business & Economics / Finance / Financial Planning

- SEL031000 — Self-Help / Personal Growth / Success

- SEL027000 — Self-Help / Motivational & Inspirational

For more information about this book and other titles by Gerry Marrs, visit:
https://www.gerrymarrspublications.com

Contents

Introduction

I n an era where financial uncertainty has become a prevailing con-
cern, "The Hidden Money Manual: Find Cash to Pay Your Bills
Now" emerges as a beacon of hope and guidance. This book is meticulously crafted for individuals who find themselves grappling with
financial dilemmas, striving to stretch their dollar further, or simply
aiming to fortify their financial future. It peels back the layers of com-
plexity surrounding personal finance, revealing practical, easy-to-im-
plement strategies to uncover hidden assets, minimize expenditures,
and sustainably increase income. Whether you're facing immediate
financial pressures or seeking to build a cushion for unforeseen circumstances, this manual is designed to elevate your financial literacy
and empower you to take control of your financial destiny. With an
emphasis on actionable advice and real-world applicability, "The Hidden Money Manual" serves not only as a resource but as a companion
in your journey towards financial stability and independence.

The Hidden Money Concept: An Exploration

At its core, the "Hidden Money Concept" revolves around the idea
that there are untapped financial resources and opportunities within

everyone's reach, yet often overlooked. The concept challenges the traditional perception that additional income can only come from working more hours or securing a higher paying job. Instead, it introduces a paradigm shift, encouraging individuals to explore unconventional avenues for financial growth and stability. This includes optimizing existing assets, reducing wasteful expenditures, and leveraging low-risk side ventures. The approach is grounded in the belief that by applying creativity, diligence, and a strategic mindset, anyone can reveal and capitalize on these hidden streams of income.

One of the key components of the Hidden Money Concept is financial mindfulness—a principle that calls for a more conscious and intentional approach to managing personal finances. This involves not only tracking expenses and income but also critically analyzing spending habits, identifying non-essential expenditures that can be eliminated or reduced. The concept underscores the importance of budgeting not as a restrictive practice but as a tool for empowerment, enabling individuals to reallocate resources towards more meaningful and productive uses. By adopting a mindset of financial mindfulness, readers are encouraged to make informed decisions that align with their long-term financial goals and well-being.

Another vital aspect addressed in the manual is the opportunity to generate income through various side hustles and passive income streams. The book provides a comprehensive guide on how to identify one's skills and interests, and how to monetize them without compromising one's primary source of income. It explores a range of possibilities, from freelance work and online sales to investment in low-risk financial instruments. The emphasis is on finding a balance between effort, reward, and risk, ensuring that any additional income activity aligns with the individual's lifestyle and financial objectives.

Lastly, "The Hidden Money Manual" emphasizes the significance of adopting a proactive approach towards financial education and planning. It advocates for continuous learning, staying abreast of financial news and trends, and being open to advice from financial experts. By doing so, individuals not only become more adept at navigating their financial landscapes but also at identifying and seizing opportunities for growth and improvement. This aspect of the concept is particularly crucial in fostering a resilient financial mindset, capable of adapting to challenges and making the most out of available resources.

Through these principles, "The Hidden Money Manual" aims to dispel the myths surrounding personal finance management, offering readers a practical and optimistic roadmap to financial autonomy and prosperity. By understanding and applying the Hidden Money Concept, individuals are empowered to transform their financial situations, creating a future that is not only secure but also abundant with possibilities.

Financial Literacy: The Key to Unlocking Hidden Funds

Financial literacy is often heralded as the golden key to unlocking a kingdom where financial stability and growth are not just aspirational goals but achievable realities. It encompasses understanding how money works in the real world, how to manage it, invest it, and save it for future needs. In an era where financial landscapes are evolving rapidly, bolstered by digital advancements and global market fluctuations, being financially literate is more than just beneficial—it's essential. The crux of financial literacy lies not just in grasping basic financial concepts but in applying this knowledge to make informed, prudent decisions about daily financial affairs.

The Hidden Money Manual underscores the importance of this literacy by guiding individuals through the labyrinth of financial jargon and complex investment vehicles with striking clarity and simplicity. It serves as a beacon for those who find the realms of budgeting, savings, investing, and managing debt overwhelming. By breaking down complex concepts into digestible, actionable steps, the manual aims to imbue readers with the confidence to take charge of their financial futures. Engaging with this material opens the door to a new perspective, challenging the myth that one needs to be born into wealth to achieve financial security and prosperity.

Yet, financial literacy is not just about personal gain; it's about contributing to a broader economic stability and prosperity. Educated financial decisions made by individuals can lead to a healthier economy by reducing personal debt, increasing savings, and investing in businesses that drive economic growth. This ripple effect means that the benefits of one's financial literacy extend beyond the individual, supporting a stronger, more resilient economy. "The Hidden Money Manual" subtly emphasizes this interconnectedness, urging readers to consider the broader impact of their financial choices.

Beyond the immediate benefits, financial literacy plays a pivotal role in achieving long-term goals, such as retirement planning and legacy building. It's about planting trees under whose shade one does not plan to sit. Understanding how to grow and protect one's wealth ensures that the benefits of one's hard work and financial prudence will be felt by future generations. In essence, "The Hidden Money Manual" is not just a guide to financial well-being; it's a roadmap to creating a legacy of financial wisdom and security that can be passed down through generations, fostering a cycle of prosperity that transcends the present to benefit the future.

The Structure of This Manual

"The Hidden Money Manual" is structured to be both easy to understand and comprehensive in its approach to financial education. It
begins with the basics of financial literacy, explaining concepts such as
budgeting, saving, and the importance of starting early. The manual
aims to demystify the financial world, making it accessible to people
from all walks of life. Each chapter builds on the previous one, gradually introducing more complex topics such as investing, tax planning,
and risk management. This progression allows readers to develop a
strong foundation of knowledge before tackling the more advanced
aspects of managing their finances.

One of the standout features of the manual is its practicality. It
doesn't just educate; it empowers. The book contains actionable steps
that readers can take immediately to start improving their financial
situation. From simple daily habits to long-term investment strategies,
there is something in it for everyone. Whether you're a college student
looking to manage student loans or a mid-career professional planning
for retirement, the manual offers tailored advice that can be applied to
various life stages.

Furthermore, the manual addresses the psychological aspects of
financial decision-making. It explores common cognitive biases and
emotional factors that can lead to poor financial choices, such as impulse spending or the fear of investing. By bringing these issues to
light, the book encourages readers to develop a healthier relationship
with money, one that is driven by informed decisions rather than
fleeting emotions or societal pressures.

Lastly, "The Hidden Money Manual" places a strong emphasis on
ethical financial practices and the importance of giving back. It discusses how financial prosperity can and should be leveraged for social

good, whether through philanthropy, ethical investing, or supporting businesses that prioritize sustainability. It paints a vision of financial success that is not just about personal gain but about contributing to the welfare of the community and the planet. Through its comprehensive and thoughtful approach, the manual does not just aim to produce wealthier individuals but to cultivate a generation of financially literate citizens who are conscious of the wider impact of their economic decisions.

How to Navigate and Utilize This Book

To efficiently harness the wealth of information contained within "The Hidden Money Manual," readers are advised to approach the book not just as a one-time read but as a lifelong resource. Begin by identifying the chapters or sections that most directly relate to your current financial situation or objectives. For example, if you are a recent graduate burdened with student loans, the sections on debt management and budgeting will be of immediate use. Conversely, established professionals might find more value in advanced investment strategies or advice on ethical investing.

Adapting the principles outlined in the manual to your personal financial goals requires both dedication and patience. It's beneficial to set clear, achievable objectives and to periodically review and adjust these as your financial situation evolves. Implementing the strategies discussed in the book might involve making significant changes to your spending habits, investment choices, or even your approach to work and earnings. Remember, the path to financial literacy and independence is a marathon, not a sprint.

The psychological aspects of financial decision-making introduced in the manual deserve special attention. Readers should strive to develop an awareness of their own biases and emotional triggers when it comes to money. Engaging in reflective practices such as journaling about spending decisions or discussing financial goals with a trusted friend can help illuminate patterns of behavior that deviate from one's financial plans. This self-awareness is crucial for overcoming obstacles to financial stability and success.

Lastly, "The Hidden Money Manual" challenges readers to think beyond their personal financial success to consider how they can contribute to the broader community. This ethos of financial prosperity coupled with social responsibility may inspire readers to pursue philanthropic activities, support ethical businesses, or engage in responsible investing. By applying the principles of the manual not only to amass wealth but also to wield it for the greater good, readers can contribute to a more equitable and sustainable world.

The Importance of Proactive Financial Management

Proactive financial management, as outlined in "The Hidden Money Manual," requires a disciplined and educated approach. The transition from passive to active engagement with one's finances can be a significant shift, demanding not just a change in habits but also a transformation in mindset. It begins with the simple act of taking stock of current financial health—assessing income, debts, savings, and investments. This initial step is crucial for setting the stage for more educated decisions about budgeting, saving, and investing. It involves creating a plan that aligns with personal and professional goals while being flexible enough to adapt to life's unpredictable changes.

To truly embody proactive financial management, individuals must become savvy consumers and investors. This implies a thorough understanding of the financial products available, from savings accounts with favorable interest rates to investment vehicles that match one's risk tolerance and time horizon. Educating oneself about these options, potentially with the help of a financial advisor, can demystify the often complex financial markets. It is also about staying informed about broader economic conditions that might affect personal finances, such as inflation rates, housing markets, and employment trends. In essence, proactive financial management involves constant learning and adaptation.

Another significant aspect is the development of a strong savings and investment strategy. The principles laid out in "The Hidden Money Manual" emphasize the power of compounding interest over time, which underscores the importance of starting to save and invest early. However, it's not solely about putting money away; it's about investing wisely. Diversification across different asset classes can mitigate risk, and regularly reviewing and adjusting one's investment portfolio ensures alignment with changing financial goals and market conditions.

Lastly, proactive financial management extends beyond personal gain to encompass a broader, community-oriented perspective. The manual encourages readers to consider how their financial decisions impact society at large. This could mean investing in socially responsible funds that prioritize ethical business practices or contributing to charities and causes that promote fiscal literacy and economic empowerment. By weaving social responsibility into the fabric of personal financial management, individuals can create not only personal wealth but also contribute to a healthier, more equitable economy. Through a comprehensive and intentional approach, proactive financial management empowers individuals to take control of their financial future, ensuring stability and success for themselves and contributing positively to the community around them.

Common Financial Challenges and Solutions

Facing financial challenges is a common experience for many individuals and families. It's an integral part of managing one's personal finances. From unforeseen medical expenses to the sudden loss of income, these hurdles can stress financial plans and savings. Identifying and acknowledging these challenges is the first step towards finding viable solutions. Education on personal finance and awareness of potential pitfalls can significantly empower individuals to anticipate and navigate these obstacles more effectively.

One prevalent challenge is debt accumulation, often resulting from credit cards, loans, or unforeseen expenses. Managing and eventually overcoming debt requires a comprehensive strategy that may include consolidating debts to secure lower interest rates, implementing stricter budgeting measures, and prioritizing debt payments. Some individuals might find it helpful to seek professional financial advice or services that specialize in debt management. The key is to avoid allowing debt to accumulate further while methodically reducing the existing financial burden.

Another significant challenge lies in saving for the future, be it for retirement, education, or emergencies. The concept of "paying yourself first" can be a practical approach; it involves setting aside a certain percentage of income for savings before addressing other expenses. Technology can aid in this endeavor, with various apps and tools designed to automate savings and help track financial goals. Investing in retirement accounts like 401(k)s or IRAs, exploring educational savings plans, and maintaining an emergency fund are concrete steps towards securing financial stability.

Lastly, a common impediment to effective financial management is a lack of financial literacy. Many individuals feel overwhelmed by the complexities of financial planning, investing, and navigating the financial markets. Investing in financial education, whether through formal education, self-study, or professional advice, can demystify the process and provide valuable insights. Engaging with community resources, attending workshops, and utilizing online platforms can enhance one's understanding and confidence in managing personal finances. Overcoming challenges in personal finance is not only about immediate solutions but also about building a foundation of knowledge and habits that ensures long-term financial health and stability.

Identifying Your Financial Goals

Identifying personal financial goals is a critical step towards achieving financial health and independence. Goals may range from short-term objectives, such as saving for a vacation or paying off credit card debt, to long-term aspirations like ensuring a comfortable retirement or buying a home. The process begins with a thorough evaluation of one's current financial situation, including income, debts, expenses, and savings. This evaluation helps in setting realistic and achievable goals that are aligned with one's financial capacity and life aspirations.

Once goals are identified, prioritizing them becomes essential. Not all financial objectives can be pursued simultaneously, especially when resources are limited. Prioritization helps in focusing efforts and resources on the most critical goals, such as securing an emergency fund or paying off high-interest debts, before moving on to less urgent ones. This approach not only streamlines financial planning but also provides a clear roadmap for achieving specific financial milestones.

Developing a concrete plan to achieve these financial goals is the next pivotal step. This plan should outline specific actions, timelines, and strategies. For short-term goals, creating a detailed budget that allocates funds towards the goal each month might be sufficient. For long-term goals, strategies may include regular investments, increasing income sources, or leveraging tax-advantaged savings accounts. Utilizing financial planning tools and consulting with professionals can provide insights and strategies customized to individual financial situations.

Finally, monitoring progress and being flexible to adjust plans as necessary is vital to staying on track toward achieving financial goals. Life events, economic shifts, and changes in personal circumstances can impact one's financial standing and priorities. Regularly reviewing financial plans and goals, at least annually, helps in making necessary adjustments to strategies, ensuring that financial objectives remain attainable and aligned with one's evolving financial landscape. Recognizing achievements and learning from setbacks can also motivate continued progress towards financial independence and security.

Success Stories: From Financial Stress to Stability

Emma's journey from financial stress to stability started shortly after she graduated from college, burdened with a significant amount of student loan debt and credit card debt. Fresh out of college, Emma found herself in a precarious financial situation, exacerbated by the high cost of living in her city. Recognizing the need for a change, she began by setting clear, realistic goals. Her primary objective was to create an emergency fund, intending to cover three to six months of living expenses, and to devise a plan to aggressively pay down her high-interest debts.

To achieve her financial goals, Emma focused on developing a detailed budget that accounted for all her expenses, prioritizing her debts from highest to lowest interest rates. She adopted the debt snowball method, which involves paying off debts in order from smallest to largest, gaining momentum as each balance is paid off. To supplement her income, Emma took on freelance projects and participated in the gig economy, directing any additional earnings towards her debt. She also utilized financial planning tools and apps to track her progress and stay motivated.

Throughout her financial turnaround, Emma encountered several unexpected challenges, including a temporary job loss and unexpected medical expenses. However, her emergency fund served as a critical safety net during these times, preventing her from accruing additional debt. By being flexible and willing to adjust her financial plan, Emma was able to navigate these setbacks without derailing her progress towards financial stability. Her strategy of regularly reviewing and adjusting her financial plan, based on her changing needs and circumstances, proved invaluable.

Emma's story is a testament to the power of determined financial planning, discipline, and resilience. After several years of commitment to her financial plan, she successfully paid off all her debts and built a robust emergency fund. Today, Emma continues to set new financial goals, including saving for a down payment on her first home and investing for retirement. Her transition from financial stress to stability underscores the importance of setting clear goals, developing a strategic plan, monitoring progress, and being adaptable. Emma's success story serves as an inspiration to others facing financial challenges, demonstrating that with the right approach, financial security is within reach.

Planning Your Financial Journey with This Manual

This manual is designed to guide you through the intricacies of managing your finances with wisdom and foresight, much like Emma did in her inspiring story. The first step in your financial journey is to establish clear, achievable goals. Whether it's paying off debt, saving for a home, or planning for retirement, having a clear target in mind gives you a destination to strive towards. It's essential to be realistic and specific with your goals to make them truly attainable. Start by setting short-term targets that will pave the way to your long-term aspirations.

Next, creating a comprehensive and realistic budget is crucial. A budget is more than just tracking income and expenses; it's a tool for making informed financial decisions and staying on course towards your goals. To begin, list all sources of income, including regular paychecks, any side gigs, and passive income streams. Then, categorize your expenses starting with necessities like housing, food, and transportation, followed by debts and savings. Remember, a good budget is not set in stone; it's a living document that should be reviewed and adjusted regularly to reflect changes in your financial situation.

Building an emergency fund is another pillar of financial stability, as demonstrated in Emma's story. Life is unpredictable, and unforeseen expenses can arise at any time. An emergency fund acts as a financial buffer that can help you avoid debt during tough times. Financial experts often recommend saving enough to cover three to six months' worth of living expenses. Start small if necessary and gradually increase your savings over time. This fund should be easily accessible, but separate from your regular checking account to avoid temptation.

Lastly, tackling debt head-on is essential for achieving financial freedom. High-interest debts, such as credit card balances, can quickly spiral out of control if not addressed. Consider strategies such as the snowball method, where you pay off the smallest debts first to build momentum, or the avalanche method, focusing on debts with the highest interest rates. Whichever strategy you choose, the key is consistency and dedication. Just like Emma, you may face challenges along the way, but with a solid plan and the flexibility to adapt, financial stability is an achievable goal.

In conclusion, this manual is designed to be a roadmap for your financial wellness. By setting clear goals, maintaining a realistic budget, building an emergency fund, and tackling debt strategically, you can emulate Emma's success. Remember, the journey to financial stability is a marathon, not a sprint. With determination and discipline, you can achieve lasting financial health and security.

Checklist for Financial Preparedness

To further solidify your path towards financial preparedness, consider the importance of continuous education and staying informed about financial trends and tools. The world of finance is constantly evolving, with new products, services, and technologies emerging. By keeping abreast of these changes, you can make informed decisions that align with your financial goals. For example, understanding the basics of investments and the role they can play in your financial strategy could open new avenues for income and wealth building. Whether it's reading financial news, books, or enrolling in courses, investing in your financial education is a step towards empowerment and independence.

Another crucial aspect of financial preparedness is protecting your assets and income. This can be achieved through appropriate insurance coverage. Often overlooked, insurance is a key component of a comprehensive financial plan. It safeguards against unexpected events that could otherwise derail your financial progress. Evaluating your need for health, life, disability, and property insurance ensures that you and your family are protected against life's uncertainties. Regularly review your insurance policies to ascertain they meet your current needs and adjust them as necessary.

In addition to safeguarding your assets, it's imperative to consider the future by planning for retirement. The earlier you start, the more you can benefit from the power of compound interest. Many people underestimate the amount of money they will need in retirement. Contributing to retirement accounts such as 401(k)s, IRAs, or Roth IRAs helps ensure that your golden years are comfortable and secure. Take advantage of any employer matching programs, as this is essentially free money that can significantly boost your retirement savings.

Finally, don't underestimate the value of professional advice. Financial planners and advisors can provide personalized guidance based on your unique financial situation and goals. They can help you navigate complex financial decisions, optimize your tax strategy, and adapt your plan to changing circumstances. While there is a cost associated with professional financial advice, the investment can be worthwhile, helping you avoid costly mistakes and making the most of your financial resources. Remember, achieving financial preparedness is not a one-time effort but a continual process that requires attention, adaptability, and action.

Chapter One

Diagnosing Your Financial Health

Understanding and managing one's financial health is akin to maintaining physical fitness; it necessitates a regular check-up and adherence to healthy habits. In this chapter, we explore the concept of diagnosing your financial health—a critical first step toward achieving financial well-being and security. Just as a doctor's check-up provides a snapshot of your physical health, a financial health check-up helps gauge your current financial status, revealing areas of strength and pinpointing potential vulnerabilities. This process involves evaluating various dimensions of your finances, including savings, debt, expenditures, and investments, to ascertain how well they align with your short-term and long-term financial goals. Through practical advice and actionable strategies, this chapter aims to equip you with the necessary tools to assess and improve your financial condition effectively. By understanding where you stand financially, you can make informed decisions that pave the way for a prosperous and secure future. Whether you're just starting to manage your personal finances or looking to refine your approach, this chapter serves as a foundational guide to better financial health.

How to Assess Your Financial Status Accurately

Assessing your financial status accurately is the linchpin of personal financial management. It begins with the gathering of all your financial documents, including bank statements, investment accounts, monthly bills, credit card statements, and any loans or mortgages you might have. This comprehensive view allows you to see the complete picture of your finances in one sweep. Next, creating a detailed list of your assets (what you own) and liabilities (what you owe) will enable you to calculate your net worth. Your net worth is a critical measure of your financial health at any given time, providing a clear indicator of where you stand financially and serving as a baseline for measuring progress over time.

To further refine your financial assessment, scrutinize your income and expenses. This involves tracking your monthly income from all sources against your monthly expenses, which include fixed obligations such as rent or mortgage payments, utilities, and variable costs like groceries, entertainment, and personal spending. Identifying the difference between these figures can illuminate your financial flexibility, revealing how much of your income is truly available for saving, investing, or paying off debt. The goal is to have a positive cash flow, where your income exceeds your expenditures, allowing for financial growth and stability.

Debt evaluation is another crucial aspect of understanding your financial status. It's important to differentiate between 'good' debt, such as a mortgage or student loans, which can represent an investment in your future, and 'bad' debt, like high-interest credit card debt, which can significantly hinder your financial progress. Listing all debts in order of interest rate or balance can help formulate a strategy for repayment that minimizes interest paid over time and accelerates the path to being debt-free.

Finally, assessing your financial preparedness for emergencies and long-term goals is essential. An emergency fund, ideally covering 3-6 months of living expenses, offers a safety net against unforeseen financial distress. Additionally, evaluating your savings and investment progress toward long-term objectives, such as retirement, education funds, or major purchases, can ensure you're on track to meet those goals. Undertaking this comprehensive financial health checkup, while daunting, is a vital first step in taking control of your financial destiny, paving the way for enhanced financial security and peace of mind.

Introduction to Budgeting Apps and Their Benefits

In today's fast-paced world, managing finances has become increasingly complex, yet the importance of maintaining a strong and healthy financial standing has never been more crucial. To aid in this endeavor, a variety of budgeting apps have emerged, offering users an intuitive and accessible means to take control of their finances. These apps serve as powerful tools, designed to simplify the tasks of tracking expenditures, creating budgets, and planning for financial goals.

One of the primary benefits of using budgeting apps is the real-time monitoring of income and expenses. By linking directly to users' bank accounts and credit cards, these apps provide an up-to-the-minute view of financial transactions, categorizing them to offer insights into spending patterns. This immediate feedback loop enables users to identify areas where they may be overspending and adjust their habits accordingly. Furthermore, budgeting apps often feature customizable alerts and notifications to warn users when they're approaching set spending limits, effectively preventing potential overspending.

Another significant advantage of budgeting apps is their role in goal setting and tracking. Users can input their financial objectives, such as saving for a down payment on a home, paying off credit card debt, or establishing an emergency fund. The app then creates a plan, breaking down these large goals into manageable, incremental steps. It tracks progress over time, offering encouragement and adjusting strategies as needed to keep users on track. This aspect of budgeting apps not only supports financial planning but also motivates users through visual progress indicators and achievements.

Lastly, budgeting apps offer the convenience of accessibility. With features available on smartphones, tablets, and computers, users can manage their finances anytime and from anywhere. This level of accessibility ensures that individuals can make informed financial decisions in real-time, such as evaluating the affordability of a purchase while shopping. Additionally, many budgeting apps include educational resources and personalized tips based on users' spending habits and financial goals, further empowering them to improve their financial literacy and making complex financial concepts more digestible.

In conclusion, the integration of budgeting apps into daily financial management can significantly enhance an individual's ability to maintain and grow their financial health. By offering real-time tracking, goal setting and progress monitoring, and unparalleled convenience, these tools democratize financial planning, making it accessible and achievable for a broader audience. Whether for individuals seeking to get a better handle on their spending or for those striving towards ambitious financial goals, budgeting apps represent a critical step towards financial empowerment and stability.

Online Calculators for Debt Management

Online calculators for debt management emerge as another indispensable tool in the realm of personal finance, complementing budgeting apps by providing users with specific insights into their debt repayment strategies. These calculators are designed to help individuals understand the most efficient way to pay off debts, be it credit cards, student loans, or mortgages. By inputting key details about their debts, such as the amount owed, interest rates, and monthly payment amounts, users can obtain a personalized plan that outlines how long it will take to be debt-free under various scenarios.

The flexibility and comprehensiveness of online debt calculators empower users to explore multiple repayment strategies. For instance, the debt snowball method focuses on paying off debts from smallest to largest, building momentum as each balance is cleared. Conversely, the debt avalanche method prioritizes debts with the highest interest rates first, potentially saving users significant amounts in interest payments over time. By visualizing these strategies through calculators, individuals can make informed decisions about which approach aligns best with their financial goals and personal preferences.

Another significant advantage of using online calculators for debt management is their ability to highlight the impact of additional payments. Even small increases in monthly payments can significantly reduce the repayment period and total interest paid. This feature encourages users to find extra money in their budgets—perhaps identified through the use of budgeting apps—to allocate toward debt repayment. This synergistic use of financial tools can accelerate the path to financial freedom.

Ultimately, online calculators for debt management and budgeting apps together provide a holistic approach to personal finance management. By offering detailed insights into spending, saving, and debt repayment, these digital tools equip individuals with the knowledge and strategies needed to take control of their finances. Whether the goal is to get out of debt, save for a significant purchase, or simply gain a better understanding of personal finance, leveraging these resources can lead to more informed decisions and a healthier financial future.

Creating a Personalized Financial Tracking System

Creating a personalized financial tracking system is critical for managing one's finances effectively. To start, individuals should consider utilizing both budgeting apps and debt management calculators as a centralized system for tracking expenses, incomes, investments, and debts. This integrated approach ensures a comprehensive overview of personal finances, allowing for real-time updates and adjustments. By consolidating financial data in one place, individuals can eliminate the guesswork in budgeting and debt repayment strategies, making financial management less daunting and more systematic.

The first step in creating this system involves selecting the right tools that match one's financial goals and personal preferences. There are myriad financial applications available, each offering different features such as expense tracking, investment monitoring, or debt planning. It's essential to choose apps and calculators that not only have a user-friendly interface but also provide robust data security to protect financial information. Integrating these tools with banking and credit accounts can automate much of the data entry process, ensuring that financial records are always current and accurate.

Once the tools are in place, the next step is to establish a routine for monitoring and updating the system. Regularly checking financial status helps in identifying spending patterns, tracking progress towards debt repayment, and adjusting budget categories as necessary. Monthly reviews allow for the fine-tuning of financial strategies, ensuring that individuals stay on track with their goals. It's also a good time to assess the effectiveness of the chosen tools and make any necessary changes or upgrades.

Finally, the success of a personalized financial tracking system hinges on the individual's commitment to financial discipline and continuous learning. Educating oneself about personal finance management, exploring new strategies for saving and investing, and staying informed about financial news and trends can significantly augment the effectiveness of financial tools. Additionally, setting clear, achievable goals, whether it's becoming debt-free, saving for a down payment on a house, or building an emergency fund, provides motivation and guidance in financial decision-making processes. With the right tools, regular maintenance, and a proactive approach to personal finance, individuals can achieve financial stability and freedom.

Setting Realistic Financial Goals

Setting realistic financial goals is an integral step toward achieving financial stability and independence. It requires a detailed understanding of one's current financial situation, including income, expenses, debts, and investments. By realistically assessing these elements, individuals can set achievable goals that are both inspiring and practical. Financial goals should stretch one's capabilities without causing undue stress or setting the stage for disappointment. This delicate balance ensures that individuals remain motivated and engaged in their financial planning efforts.

In the process of setting financial goals, prioritization plays a crucial role. Not all financial objectives can be pursued simultaneously with equal intensity, especially when resources are limited. Thus, distinguishing between short-term and long-term goals is essential. Short-term goals, like saving for a vacation or paying off a small credit card debt, are usually achievable within a year and can provide quick, gratifying wins that bolster confidence. Long-term goals, such as saving for retirement or a child's college fund, require a more extended commitment and often demand sacrifices in the present for future benefits.

A key strategy in achieving financial goals is the SMART criteria—Specific, Measurable, Achievable, Relevant, and Time-bound. Goals defined using this framework have a higher chance of being realized. For example, instead of vaguely aiming to "save more money," a SMART goal would be "to save $200 every month for the next year to create a $2400 emergency fund." This method not only specifies the amount and timeframe but also includes actionable steps to achieve the goal, making it easier to monitor progress and adjust actions as needed.

Lastly, accountability and flexibility are crucial in navigating the path towards financial goals. Life's unpredictability means that circumstances can change, impacting one's ability to meet initially set targets. Regularly reviewing and adjusting goals ensures they remain relevant and attainable. Sharing these goals with a trusted friend, family member, or financial advisor can also provide an added layer of accountability, encouraging commitment and perseverance. In the end, the success in reaching financial goals lies not just in meticulous planning but also in the ability to adapt and persist amidst challenges.

The Role of Emergency Funds

Establishing an emergency fund is an essential step in achieving financial security. It acts as a financial safety net designed to cover unexpected expenses without the need to incur debt or dip into long-term savings. Emergency funds can mitigate the stress and financial strain caused by sudden life events such as job loss, medical emergencies, or essential home repairs. Financial advisors often recommend setting aside three to six months' worth of living expenses in an easily accessible account. This ensures that individuals or families can maintain their standard of living during periods of financial uncertainty.

The process of building an emergency fund requires discipline and a strategic approach. Starting small and gradually increasing the savings amount can make the process less daunting. Automating transfers to a dedicated savings account can ensure consistent growth of the fund over time. It's also wise to review and adjust the contribution amounts as financial situations change, such as after receiving a raise or paying off debt. Celebrating milestones along the way can serve as motivation to continue building the fund until the desired goal is reached.

Choosing the right account for an emergency fund is crucial to ensure that the funds are both secure and accessible. High-yield savings accounts, money market accounts, or short-term certificates of deposit can offer higher interest rates compared to traditional savings accounts, allowing the emergency fund to grow while remaining liquid. It's important to select an account with no or low fees and convenient access so that the money can be withdrawn without penalties when needed.

Finally, maintaining the emergency fund is an ongoing process. Regularly reviewing and adjusting the fund size to match current living expenses, lifestyle changes, or changes in economic circumstances is necessary. Also, if the fund is used during an emergency, replenishing it should become a priority to ensure that the safety net remains intact for future needs. A well-maintained emergency fund not only provides financial security but also grants peace of mind, allowing individuals and families to face unexpected challenges with confidence.

Prioritizing Expenses: Needs vs. Wants

In the realm of financial planning, distinguishing between needs and wants is a fundamental step towards achieving a balanced and sustainable budget. Needs are expenses that are necessary for survival and basic well-being, such as housing, food, healthcare, and transportation. Wants, on the other hand, are discretionary expenses that enhance our quality of life but are not essential for living, like dining out, entertainment, and luxury items. For a financially healthy lifestyle, it is crucial to prioritize needs over wants, ensuring that the essential expenses are covered before allocating money towards less critical expenditures.

Creating a budget is the most effective way to manage the delicate balance between needs and wants. This involves listing all sources of income and identifying all expenses, categorizing them into needs and wants. By doing so, one can have a clear picture of their financial situation, which aids in making informed decisions about where to cut back if necessary. A budget provides a roadmap for where money should go, allowing for adjustments to be made to ensure that saving goals are met and that there is enough to cover the basics.

One practical strategy for prioritizing expenses is the 50/30/20 rule, which suggests spending approximately 50% of after-tax income on needs, 30% on wants, and allocating 20% to savings and debt repayment. This guideline serves as a starting point for creating a balanced budget, emphasizing the importance of meeting essential needs while still allowing for enjoyment and savings. Adjustments can be made based on personal financial goals and circumstances, but the principle of living within one's means remains constant.

Finally, regularly reviewing and adjusting the budget is vital for maintaining financial health. Life circumstances and financial situations can change, necessitating a reassessment of what constitutes a need versus a want. For example, a gym membership may be considered a want, but if it significantly contributes to one's mental and physical health, it might become a need. By staying vigilant and flexible, individuals can continue to make informed choices about their spending, ensuring that they can meet their current needs, enjoy their wants responsibly, and build a secure financial future.

Understanding Your Credit Score

Understanding your credit score is a critical aspect of managing your financial health. A credit score is a numerical representation based on a level analysis of a person's credit files, to represent the creditworthiness of an individual. A higher score indicates better credit health and can significantly affect your ability to obtain loans, the interest rates you will be offered, and even your eligibility for certain jobs or rental properties. Consequently, it becomes essential to grasp how these scores are calculated and the steps one can take to improve them.

Credit scores are primarily influenced by factors such as your payment history, the amount of debt you carry, the length of your credit history, the types of credit you use, and recent credit inquiries. Payment history is the most critical component, accounting for about 35% of your score. It reflects whether you make payments on time, how often you miss them, and if any debts have been sent to collection agencies. Ensuring timely payments on all debts is a straightforward strategy to maintain or improve your credit score.

The debt-to-credit ratio, representing the amount of credit you are using compared to your total available credit, also significantly impacts your credit score. Experts recommend keeping this ratio below 30% to be viewed favorably by creditors. Additionally, the length of your credit history, accounting for 15% of your score, implies that individuals with a longer credit history are generally seen as less risky compared to those with a short credit history. Thus, it's beneficial to maintain older credit accounts in good standing.

Lastly, understanding the implications of hard inquiries on your credit report is crucial. Each time you apply for a loan or a credit card, a hard inquiry is made, which can slightly lower your credit score. To minimize this impact, limit the number of new accounts or loans you apply for within a short period. Regularly monitoring your credit report for inaccuracies and unauthorized activities can also prevent potential damage to your score. By managing these aspects of your credit, you can work towards building a robust credit history that will serve your financial interests in the long term.

Tools for Regular Financial Review and Adjustment

Navigating the world of personal finance requires continual learning and adjustment. One of the first steps in ensuring your financial health is the utilization of tools that enable regular review and fine-tuning of your financial strategy. This includes not only tracking expenses and income but also keeping an eye on your credit score and understanding how different financial decisions impact it. Many personal finance apps and websites offer integrated tools that can help you monitor all these facets in one place, providing insights and alerts that can guide your financial decisions.

Budgeting tools form the backbone of financial planning, offering the clarity needed to make informed decisions about your spending. Setting up a budget allows you to allocate your income toward different categories, ensuring that you live within your means while setting aside money for savings and investments. Digital budgeting tools often come with the capability to categorize transactions automatically, making it easier to stick to your budget and identify areas where you might be overspending.

Credit monitoring services are another essential tool for anyone looking to maintain or improve their financial standing. These services keep track of your credit score and report, alerting you to any changes that could indicate potential fraud or errors that need to be disputed. Some services even offer advice on how to improve your credit score based on the current status of your credit report. Regular monitoring can help you understand how your financial behaviors affect your credit over time, which is invaluable for long-term financial health.

Finally, investment tools can aid individuals in making their money work for them. Whether you're a seasoned investor or new to the game, these tools can offer insights into your portfolio, suggest adjustments, and even automate some of the investment processes. They range from simple robo-advisors that manage investments based on your risk tolerance to more sophisticated platforms that offer detailed analysis on various investment opportunities. By leveraging these tools, individuals can strive towards achieving their financial goals, whether that's saving for a major purchase, funding education, or planning for retirement.

Establishing a Financial Health Check Routine

Establishing a regular financial health check routine is akin to routine maintenance for your car – it's essential for ensuring everything runs smoothly and prevents potential issues from becoming severe. Setting aside a specific time each month to review your finances can provide you with a clear snapshot of where you stand, allowing you to make informed decisions moving forward. This routine should include analyzing spending, reviewing savings and investment progress, checking credit reports, and re-evaluating financial goals.

When reviewing your spending, take note of where your money is going and compare it to your budget. Identify any areas where you may be overspending and consider making adjustments to align your spending with your financial goals. This might involve cutting back on non-essential expenses or finding more cost-effective alternatives for necessary expenditures. Regularly analyzing your spending patterns can also help you catch any fraudulent transactions early, keeping your financial information secure.

In terms of savings and investments, evaluating your progress towards your goals is crucial. Ensure you're making the most of your investment tools and that your portfolio aligns with your current risk tolerance and financial objectives. If you're not seeing the returns you expected, it might be time to reassess your investment strategies. Additionally, checking your emergency fund to ensure it covers several months of expenses can provide peace of mind and financial stability in case of unforeseen circumstances.

Finally, regularly monitoring your credit report and score is vital for maintaining good financial health. Errors on your credit report can negatively impact your credit score, making it harder to secure loans with favorable interest rates. If you find any inaccuracies, dispute them promptly. Also, use this time to learn more about how your financial behavior influences your credit score. By understanding the factors that impact your score, such as payment history and credit utilization, you can take steps to improve it, if necessary. Establishing a routine for financial health checks can empower you to maintain control over your finances and work confidently towards your long-term financial goals.

Chapter Two

Cutting Costs with Resourceful Platforms

I n Chapter 2 of "The Hidden Money Manual: Find Cash to Pay Your Bills Now," we venture into one of the most practical and immediately rewarding areas of personal finance management—cutting costs without significantly impacting your lifestyle. This chapter is dedicated to uncovering and making the best use of various resourceful platforms that can drastically reduce your monthly expenses. From little-known discount services to subscription management tools, we guide you through a curated selection of platforms designed to save money on everyday expenses such as groceries, utilities, subscriptions, and more. Our aim is to not only introduce you to these cost-cutting allies but to also provide you with step-by-step instructions on how to effectively integrate them into your financial strategy. By the end of this chapter, you will be equipped with the knowledge to leverage these platforms to make more informed purchasing decisions,

optimize your spending, and allocate your resources more efficiently—paving the way to a more financially sustainable lifestyle.

Bill Negotiation Services: How They Work

Bill negotiation services have emerged as an invaluable tool for consumers looking to lower their monthly bills without the hassle of dealing directly with service providers. These services, staffed by experienced negotiators, work on your behalf to secure lower rates on everything from cable and internet subscriptions to utility bills. Typically,
they leverage their knowledge of industry pricing and promotions,
along with their established relationships with providers, to negotiate
better deals. The process is straightforward for the consumer: you
simply share a copy of your bill and grant them the authority to negotiate on your behalf. In exchange for their services, these companies
usually take a percentage of the savings they achieve over a set period,
making it a win-win situation; if they don't save you money, you don't
pay.

One of the critical aspects of bill negotiation services is their ability
to reduce not just one-time bills, but to potentially lower your expenses for an extended period. Many consumers are unaware of the
promotional rates or discounts they're eligible for, which can often
be applied to their accounts with a little negotiation. By enlisting the
help of these services, you not only save money in the short term
but may also enjoy reduced payments for months or even years. Additionally, these services often monitor your bills for future savings
opportunities, ensuring that you continue to pay the lowest possible
rate. This proactive approach to bill management can significantly ease
the burden on your monthly budget, allowing you to redirect those
savings towards other financial goals.

Some notable examples of bill negotiation services that have helped consumers save significantly on their monthly expenditures include **BillFixers** (http://www.billfixers.com), **Truebill** (now part of **Rocket Money** at http://www.rocketmoney.com), and **Trim** (http://www.asktrim.com). **BillFixers** offers its services to individuals and businesses alike, striving to lower monthly bills by securing better deals from service providers. **Truebill**, which has transitioned into **Rocket Money**, provides users with a multifaceted financial management platform that includes bill negotiation among its array of services to help save money. Similarly, **Trim** leverages artificial intelligence to scrutinize users' spending habits, pinpoint savings opportunities, and engage in negotiations to reduce rates for various services. Together, these platforms have saved users millions by minimizing their monthly expenses on utility bills, subscriptions, and other recurring payments.

Subscription Management Tools and Their Impact

In today's digital age, managing subscriptions has become an intricate part of our daily lives. With everything from streaming services to software subscriptions requiring monthly or annual fees, it's easy to lose track of our spending. Thankfully, a variety of subscription management tools have emerged to help consumers maintain control over their recurring expenses. These tools not only help in tracking and managing subscriptions but also in identifying unused services that can be canceled to save money.

One such tool that has garnered attention is **Subby** (http://www.subby.io), designed to centralize and streamline the process of subscription management. By allowing users to input all their subscription details into one platform, **Subby** provides a comprehensive overview of total spending, upcoming bills, and renewal dates. This visibility helps users make informed decisions about which subscriptions are valuable and which can be cut to save costs.

Another innovative platform is **Bobby** (http://www.bobbyapp.co), which focuses on simplicity and user-friendliness. With an intuitive interface, **Bobby** lets users quickly add subscriptions and set reminders for upcoming payments. This ensures that users are always aware of their financial commitments, helping them to avoid late fees and unwanted renewals. The app also supports multiple currencies, making it an ideal choice for users with international subscriptions.

Lastly, **Mint** (http://www.mint.com), while widely recognized for its budgeting tools, also offers features for tracking subscriptions. By connecting your bank accounts and credit cards, **Mint** analyzes your transactions to identify recurring payments. This feature helps users see precisely where their money is going each month, making it easier to spot subscriptions that could be eliminated to improve financial health. In addition to subscription tracking, **Mint** provides a wealth of financial management tools, from budgeting to credit monitoring, giving users a 360-degree view of their financial landscape.

Together, these tools represent a shift towards more conscious consumption and financial management, empowering users to take control of their recurring expenses. By utilizing these platforms, individuals can ensure that their money is being spent on services that offer real value, ultimately leading to better financial well-being.

Cashback Apps: Maximizing Rewards from Everyday Purchases

In the evolving landscape of personal financial management, cashback apps have emerged as a significant player, enabling users to earn rewards from their regular shopping activities. These applications work by offering a percentage of the purchase price back to the shopper, effectively providing a discount on nearly everything they buy. Such apps are not only a boon for consumers looking to save money but also for retailers seeking to attract more customers through these incentives. The concept is simple yet powerful, briditing the gap between saving and spending by turning every purchase into an opportunity for reward.

One of the leading cashback apps in the market is **Rakuten** (http ://www.rakuten.com). Rakuten partners with a wide array of retailers across various sectors, including clothing, electronics, and groceries. Users simply need to start their shopping through the Rakuten app or website to earn cashback on their purchases. The app also occasionally offers double cashback events and other special promotions, maximizing the savings potential for users. It's a win-win situation where businesses get increased patronage, and consumers enjoy reduced costs.

Another notable app in this sphere is **Ibotta** (http://www.ibotta. com), which provides a unique twist on the traditional cashback concept. Instead of a direct percentage return, Ibotta offers cash rewards on specific products at particular stores. Users need to complete simple tasks, like watching a short video or answering a survey, to unlock the cashback offers. After purchasing the qualifying items and submitting a receipt, the cash rewards are deposited into the user's Ibotta account, which can then be withdrawn to a bank account or converted into gift cards.

Honey (http://www.joinhoney.com) is yet another innovative player, primarily known for its browser extension that automatically applies coupon codes at checkout. Beyond this, Honey also offers a rewards program known as Honey Gold. While shopping online, users can earn Gold on their purchases at participating retailers. This Gold can later be redeemed for gift cards, adding an additional layer of savings. Honey's ability to search for the best deals and offer rewards makes it an indispensable tool for savvy online shoppers.

Each of these platforms underscores the growing trend towards maximized financial efficiency in everyday transactions. By leveraging technology, cashback apps are redefining the shopping experience, allowing consumers to earn rewards effortlessly. For those looking to improve their financial health, incorporating these apps into their shopping routine can be an effective strategy in saving money and making every purchase count.

Energy-Saving Tips and Tools for Homeowners

In an era where ecological sustainability and financial prudence are becoming increasingly significant, homeowners are actively seeking ways to reduce their energy consumption. Implementing energy-saving practices not only contributes to a healthier environment by decreasing emissions but also results in substantial savings on utility bills. Several strategies, tools, and technologies can aid in achieving these goals, ranging from simple behavioral adjustments to the adoption of smart home technology.

One fundamental approach is the utilization of energy-efficient appliances. Websites like Energy Star (http://www.energystar.gov) offer comprehensive guides and ratings for a wide array of household appliances. From refrigerators to washing machines, opting for products certified by Energy Star can lead to considerable energy savings over the products' lifetimes. These appliances are designed to use the minimum amount of energy necessary to complete their tasks, without sacrificing performance.

Another critical aspect to consider is home insulation and sealing leaks. Proper insulation helps maintain the desired temperature in your house, thereby reducing the need for heating or cooling. This, in turn, lowers energy consumption significantly. Websites such as the U.S. Department of Energy (http://www.energy.gov) provide resources and tips on how to effectively insulate and seal homes. They cover areas prone to leaks like windows, doors, and attics, as well as recommend professional energy audits to identify specific issues.

In addition to these measures, the integration of smart home technology offers a dynamic approach to energy savings. Smart thermostats, such as those offered by Nest (http://www.nest.com), and lighting solutions, accessible from platforms like Philips Hue (http://www.meethue.com), allow homeowners to control their energy use remotely and automate settings for optimum efficiency. These devices can adjust the heating, cooling, and lighting based on usage patterns and preferences, potentially leading to significant reductions in energy consumption.

By adopting a combination of these strategies, tools, and technologies, homeowners can achieve meaningful energy savings. With a wealth of resources available online, it's easier than ever to make informed decisions that contribute to a sustainable and cost-effective household.

Reducing Grocery Bills: Apps and Strategies

Reducing grocery bills is another area where technology and strategy can lead to substantial savings for households. In today's digital age, numerous apps and websites have emerged, offering coupons, price comparisons, and even cashback on purchases. Apps such as `Ibotta` (http://www.ibotta.com) and `Checkout 51` (http://www.checkout 51.com) allow users to earn cashback on select grocery items by simply uploading their purchase receipts. These platforms often update their offers weekly, providing new opportunities for savings on regular purchases.

Another effective approach is utilizing price comparison websites and apps. `Basket` (http://www.basket.com) is a notable example, enabling users to compare prices across multiple local grocery stores, ensuring they get the best deals on their shopping list. This not only saves money but also time, as it reduces the need to visit multiple stores or websites to compare prices manually.

In addition to leveraging technology, adopting certain shopping strategies can further reduce grocery bills. Planning meals in advance and sticking to a shopping list can prevent impulse buys and ensure that only necessary items are purchased. Furthermore, buying in bulk, choosing store brands over name brands, and taking advantage of sales and seasonal produce can also lead to significant savings over time.

Lastly, growing a home garden for fruits, vegetables, and herbs is an excellent way to cut costs, though it may not be feasible for everyone. Websites like `Gardener's Supply Company` (http://www.gardeners.com) offer tools, seeds, and resources to help individuals start and maintain a productive garden. Not only does this provide fresh produce right at your doorstep, but it also encourages a healthier lifestyle and reduces the environmental impact of food transportation.

By combining these advanced tools with practical shopping strategies, individuals can effectively minimize their grocery expenses while still enjoying a diverse and nutritious diet. With the wealth of resources and information available online, there's never been a better time to adopt savvy shopping habits that benefit both your wallet and the planet.

Affordable Health Care Resources

Navigating the costs of health care can be as challenging as sticking to a budget at the grocery store. However, similar to using technology and strategies to save on groceries, individuals can also employ tools and resources to manage their health care expenses more efficiently. Many online platforms and services now offer ways to compare health insurance plans, find affordable medications, and even access some health services remotely, which can substantially lower costs.

For instance, websites like `HealthCare.gov` (https://www.health care.gov) allow users to compare health insurance plans to find one that fits their budget and coverage needs. This site is particularly useful during open enrollment periods or for those experiencing qualifying life events that allow for special enrollment. Another valuable resource is `GoodRx` (https://www.goodrx.com), which provides coupons for prescriptions that can greatly reduce the cost of medications, sometimes by up to 80%.

Telehealth services have also seen a significant rise in popularity, especially in the wake of the COVID-19 pandemic. Platforms like `Teladoc` (https://www.teladoc.com) offer consultations with doctors via phone or video call, often at a fraction of the price of an in-person visit. This can be particularly cost-effective for managing chronic conditions or for instances when one needs medical advice without requiring physical examinations.

Lastly, understanding and utilizing Health Savings Accounts (HSAs) or Flexible Spending Accounts (FSAs) can lead to substantial savings. Websites like `HSA Search` (https://www.hsasearch.com) help individuals find the best HSA providers, comparing fees, interest rates, and reviews. By setting aside pre-tax income into these accounts, users can pay for medical expenses directly, effectively lowering their taxable income and saving money in the long term.

By leveraging these tools and resources, individuals can make more informed decisions about their health care, ultimately leading to better health outcomes and savings. Just as technology has revolutionized the way we shop for groceries, it has also transformed the landscape of health care, making it more accessible and affordable for everyone.

Cutting Transportation Costs

Navigating the high costs of transportation requires adopting a strategic approach that leverages technology and smart planning. The rise of ridesharing apps like `Uber` (https://www.uber.com) and `Lyft` (https://www.lyft.com) has provided a convenient and often cheaper alternative to traditional taxi services. These platforms offer various options, including carpooling features like Uber Pool and Lyft Shared, which significantly reduce the cost of rides by sharing them with other passengers headed in the same direction.

Another effective strategy for cutting transportation costs is utilizing public transportation where available. Many cities have comprehensive websites for their transit systems, such as the `MTA` (https://www.mta.info) in New York, which provide schedules, fare information, and even mobile ticketing options. For regular commuters, purchasing monthly passes can offer substantial savings over individual ride tickets. Additionally, some employers offer pre-tax programs for transit costs, further lessening the financial burden.

For those who prefer the flexibility of driving without the cost of car ownership, car-sharing services like `Zipcar` (https://www.zipcar.com) and `Turo` (https://www.turo.com) offer a solution. These platforms allow individuals to rent cars by the hour or day for one-off trips or errands, providing the convenience of a personal vehicle without the associated costs of insurance, maintenance, and parking.

Lastly, cycling and walking are not only the most cost-effective modes of transportation but also offer significant health benefits. Many cities are enhancing their biking infrastructure, creating more bike lanes and making it safer for cyclists. Websites like `BikeShare` (https://www.bikeshare.com) list community bike-sharing programs across different cities, offering an affordable and environmentally friendly option for short commutes. By exploring these alternative transportation methods, individuals can significantly reduce their transportation expenses while also contributing to a more sustainable future.

Free Entertainment Resources

Entertainment plays a vital role in our lives, offering a much-needed break from the routine of daily tasks and responsibilities. However, the cost of entertainment can quickly add up, leading many to seek out free or low-cost options. Fortunately, with the rise of digital platforms, there's a wealth of free entertainment resources available online, ranging from streaming services to virtual museum tours, which can provide countless hours of enjoyment without breaking the bank.

One outstanding source of free entertainment is the world of podcasts, with platforms like `Spotify` (https://www.spotify.com) and `Apple Podcasts` (https://www.apple.com/apple-podcasts/) offering a diverse range of shows on every topic imaginable — from history and science to comedy and storytelling. These platforms allow users to stream thousands of podcasts for free, with the option to download episodes for offline listening.

For those interested in the visual arts and history, many of the world's leading museums offer free virtual tours. The `Smithsonian National Museum of Natural History` (https://naturalhistory.si.ed

u/visit/virtual-tour) and the 'British Museum' (https://www.british museum.org/collection) allow visitors to explore their vast collections online. This not only provides a free entertainment option but also an educational one, allowing individuals to learn about cultures, art, and history from around the world.

Free streaming services such as 'Crackle' (https://www.crackle.co m) and 'Tubi' (https://www.tubi.tv) offer a wide selection of movies and TV shows across various genres. While these platforms may not have the newest releases, they boast a considerable library of content that's completely free to watch, with the only trade-off being the inclusion of advertising. For those who prefer reading, many local libraries provide access to free ebooks and audiobooks through apps like 'Libby' (https://www.libbyapp.com), making it easier than ever to access a vast range of literary works without spending a dime.

Clothing and Apparel Savings Strategies

In today's digital age, finding affordable or free sources for entertainment and education is easier than it has ever been. From music and podcasts to books and movies, numerous platforms offer a wealth of content at no cost, enabling people from all walks of life to enjoy a variety of media without straining their budgets. However, when it comes to clothing and apparel, many consumers find themselves caught in a cycle of purchasing new items regularly, driven by fast fashion trends and seasonal changes. This can significantly impact one's finances, but with a strategic approach, it is possible to save on clothing while still enjoying a diverse and modern wardrobe.

One effective strategy for saving on apparel is to utilize second-hand and thrift stores, which are treasure troves of fashion at a fraction of the retail price. Websites like 'ThredUp' (https://www.thredup.com)

and 'Poshmark' (https://www.poshmark.com) allow users to buy and sell pre-owned clothing and accessories. Not only does this approach save money, but it also promotes a more sustainable lifestyle by reducing waste and the environmental impact associated with producing new garments.

Another method to consider is the subscription box model, which can offer significant savings on high-quality apparel. Services such as 'Stitch Fix' (https://www.stitchfix.com) and 'Rent the Runway' (https://www.renttherunway.com) provide personalized clothing selections based on your style preferences and needs, allowing you to freshen up your wardrobe periodically without purchasing items at full price. While this involves a recurring cost, it can be more economical in the long run, especially for those who regularly update their wardrobe or need special occasion attire without the commitment of a full purchase.

Lastly, watching for sales and utilizing discount codes can lead to substantial savings. Many clothing retailers offer significant discounts during end-of-season sales, Black Friday, Cyber Monday, and other retail holidays. Websites like 'RetailMeNot' (https://www.retailmeno t.com) and 'Honey' (https://www.joinhoney.com) can help shoppers find coupons and promotional codes for additional savings. Signing up for newsletters from your favorite brands can also alert you to private sales and exclusive discounts, making it easier to spot deals on items you love.

By exploring these strategies, individuals can enjoy diverse and fashionable attire without overspending. The key is to combine traditional shopping habits with modern platforms and services that offer both value and convenience. Whether through smart online shopping, the reuse of pre-loved items, or making the most of subscription services and discounts, achieving a stylish wardrobe while maintaining financial health is entirely possible.

DIY and Home Improvement Savings Websites

In the realm of DIY and home improvement, the internet is an invaluable resource for finding budget-friendly ideas, materials, and tools. Tackling home projects on your own can not only be immensely satisfying but also significantly cut down on costs compared to hiring professionals for every little task. There are several websites dedicated to helping enthusiasts of all skill levels find the information and resources they need to get started and successfully complete their projects.

`Instructables` (https://www.instructables.com) is a prime example of a website that caters to the DIY community. It provides free, user-generated content in the form of detailed tutorials on a wide range of projects, from simple home repairs and decorations to more complex renovations. These step-by-step guides are often accompanied by photos and videos, making it easier for users to follow along and execute projects accurately.

Another highly recommended resource is `This Old House` (https://www.thisoldhouse.com), which offers expert advice on a wide range of topics related to home improvement. Whether it's fixing a leaky faucet or planning a full kitchen remodel, the site provides practical tips and guides that can help homeowners save money while achieving professional-quality results. It also features product reviews and recommendations, ensuring that DIYers can select the best tools and materials for their projects.

For those looking for deals on tools and materials, `The Home Depot` (https://www.homedepot.com) and `Lowe's` (https://www.lowes.com) frequently offer sales and clearance items online. Additionally, websites like `Craigslist` (https://www.craigslist.org) and `Facebook Marketplace` (https://www.facebook.com/marketplace) can be great places to find used tools and materials at a fraction of the cost. By utilizing these resources, DIY enthusiasts can keep their project budgets under control while bringing their home improvement visions to life.

Chapter Three

Discovering Hidden Income and Assets

In Chapter 3 of "The Hidden Money Manual: Find Cash to Pay Your Bills Now", we will explore the often overlooked avenues for discovering hidden income and assets. This chapter is designed as a treasure map, guiding readers through various strategies to unearth financial resources that many individuals do not realize they possess. Whether it's through untapped skill sets, undervalued possessions, or neglected financial accounts, there are myriad ways to uncover additional streams of revenue that can be pivotal in achieving short-term financial relief and long-term financial stability. This chapter not only aims to enlighten readers about potential hidden assets but also teaches them how to assess and leverage these resources effectively. We will introduce practical methods for identifying hidden income opportunities, evaluating the worth of personal belongings for possible sale or investment, and revisiting financial instruments that may be lying dormant. Each section of this chapter is meticulously crafted to ensure that by its conclusion, readers will have gained the knowledge and confidence needed to tap into these untapped resources, setting the foundation for a healthier financial future.

Guide to Using MissingMoney.com

The first step to uncovering hidden income and assets is to take inventory of your financial life. This may seem daunting, but it's a critical exercise to reveal money you might not realize you have. Begin by examining your past employment history for any unclaimed wages or pension funds. Many people leave jobs and forget about accumulated benefits that are rightfully theirs. Similarly, revisit old bank accounts, insurance policies, and investments—these could have grown in value or have unclaimed funds waiting to be withdrawn.

Another often overlooked asset is personal property that carries significant value. This includes everything from antiques and artwork to collectibles and electronic gadgets. Websites like eBay (https://www.ebay.com) and Craigslist (https://www.craigslist.org) offer platforms to sell these items, turning unused possessions into liquid assets. Additionally, consider leveraging your skills and hobbies for income. Platforms such as Etsy (https://www.etsy.com) for handmade goods, or Fiverr (https://www.fiverr.com) for freelance services, provide avenues to monetize talents you may not have considered assets.

Exploring government and financial institution resources can also reveal untapped funds. The Unclaimed.org website (http://www.unclaimed.org), overseen by the National Association of Unclaimed Property Administrators, enables users to search for unclaimed property and money from various sources like tax refunds, savings bonds, or insurance policy payouts. Similarly, the TreasuryDirect website (h

ttps://www.treasurydirect.gov) offers a guide for searching and claiming forgotten U.S. savings bonds that may be gathering dust in your
name.

Lastly, consider leveraging technology to uncover additional
streams of income. Apps and websites are available that can help track
down missing money or provide avenues for passive income. For instance, Acorns (https://www.acorns.com) rounds up your purchases
to the nearest dollar and invests the difference, potentially growing
your savings without any active effort on your part. Robo-advisors like
Betterment (https://www.betterment.com) manage your investments
using algorithms, possibly uncovering higher returns on your existing
assets. By employing these strategies and resources, you can discover
hidden income and assets that can significantly bolster your financial
stability.

How to Check for Unclaimed Assets with Unclaime d.org

Discovering hidden assets and unclaimed funds can be a game-changer
for many individuals looking to enhance their financial health. The
process of checking for unclaimed assets with Unclaimed.org is both
simple and potentially rewarding. By simply entering personal details
such as your name and state, the website sifts through databases to
identify any funds that may belong to you but have not been claimed.
This could include anything from paychecks from previous employers, dividends, or refunds that you were unaware of. Given that these
funds are just sitting there waiting to be claimed, taking the initiative
to search could lead to a pleasant financial surprise.

Understanding how these assets become "unclaimed" can also be
enlightening. Often, assets become unclaimed due to miscommu-

nication, address changes, or simply forgetting about an account or policy. Over time, these assets are turned over to state treasuries until the rightful owner or heir claims them. The longer these assets remain unclaimed, the more they accumulate, sometimes reaching significant amounts. This highlights the importance of regular checks, ensuring that all your assets are accounted for and under your control.

In addition to Unclaimed.org, TreasuryDirect.gov offers a focused search particularly for U.S. savings bonds that may have been forgotten. Many individuals receive savings bonds as gifts during childhood or as part of an investment strategy but lose track of them over the years. The TreasuryDirect website provides a methodical guide on how to search for these bonds and claim them if found. This process not only uncovers hidden funds but also reintroduces a potentially valuable asset into your financial portfolio.

Lastly, leveraging technology through apps like Acorns and services like Betterment can further augment your financial landscape by making the most out of your existing assets. These platforms offer innovative ways to invest, save, and manage money, often with minimal effort required on the user's part. From rounding up change to invest in diversified portfolios to employing algorithms for smarter investing, these technologies provide a modern approach to uncovering and growing your financial assets. In the grand scheme of things, actively searching for unclaimed assets and employing available technology can significantly contribute to financial stability and growth.

Selling Unused Items for Cash: Platforms and Tips

Turning to the topic of selling unused items for cash, the internet has sparked a revolution by providing a multitude of platforms where practically anything from the gently used to the barely touched can find a new home. This not only contributes to a more sustainable lifestyle but also adds an additional stream of income with little to no initial investment. The key to success in this venture lies in understanding the best platforms for various types of items and how to present these items to catch potential buyers' eyes.

eBay (www.ebay.com) has long been the go-to platform for selling a wide array of items, from vintage collectibles to the latest gadgets. Its auction-based system allows sellers to reach a vast audience and potentially sell items at a higher price than they might anticipate. For those looking to sell clothing, **Poshmark (www.poshmark.com)** offers a community-driven marketplace focused on fashion. Here, presentation and active engagement with the community can significantly enhance sales.

For larger items like furniture, **Craigslist (www.craigslist.org)** remains a popular choice. Its local focus reduces the complexities and costs associated with shipping, making it ideal for selling bulky items. Meanwhile, **Facebook Marketplace (www.facebook.com/marketplace)** has rapidly grown in popularity for a wide range of items, benefiting from the extensive user base of Facebook and the added trust factor of dealing with real profiles.

When selling items online, a few tips can significantly improve your outcome. Firstly, high-quality, clear photos from multiple angles and well-lit settings can make your items stand out. Including detailed descriptions and being transparent about any defects or wear and tear can build trust with potential buyers. Lastly, being responsive and courteous in communications can foster positive interactions, leading to quicker sales and even repeat buyers. By leveraging these platforms and tips, you can efficiently declutter your space while bolstering your finances.

The Gig Economy: Identifying Opportunities

The gig economy has transformed how individuals earn income, offering flexibility and a variety of opportunities outside the traditional 9-to-5 job. This sector includes freelance work, part-time jobs, and side hustles, all facilitated by digital platforms that connect service providers with those in need of their services. In the context of the digital marketplace and online sales platforms discussed above, the gig economy represents a pivotal shift towards more autonomous, technology-driven employment options.

One prominent area where the gig economy thrives is in online freelancing. Websites like **Upwork (www.upwork.com)** and **Fiverr (www.fiverr.com)** serve as platforms where individuals can offer their professional services, ranging from writing and graphic design to web development and digital marketing. These sites allow freelancers to connect with clients globally, presenting a vast market for their skills. By creating a strong profile and portfolio, freelancers can attract clients looking for high-quality work.

Another significant sector within the gig economy is ride-sharing and delivery services. Companies such as **Uber (www.uber.com)** and **Lyft (www.lyft.com)** offer ride-sharing services, allowing individuals with cars to earn money by transporting passengers. Similarly, food delivery services like **DoorDash (www.doordash.com)** and **Grubhub (www.grubhub.com)** enable people to deliver food from restaurants to customers' doorsteps. These platforms provide flexible working hours, making them an attractive option for those looking to supplement their income.

Lastly, the rise of peer-to-peer lodging services such as **Airbnb (www.airbnb.com)** has opened up new opportunities for individuals to generate income from their property. By listing a spare room or entire home, homeowners can earn money by hosting tourists or travelers. This not only provides financial benefits but also fosters cultural exchange and connection among people from different parts of the world. The gig economy, with its diverse array of opportunities, continues to redefine the landscape of work and income generation in the modern age.

Crafting and Selling: Online Marketplaces

In addition to the services mentioned above, the gig economy thrives significantly on the creative talents of individuals through online marketplaces. **Etsy (www.etsy.com)** is a prime example where artisans and crafters can sell their handmade goods, vintage items, and crafting supplies. This platform caters specifically to those who excel in arts and crafts, offering a niche market with customers who appreciate the value of unique, handcrafted products. Etsy allows creators to build a global clientele, leveraging the internet to bring traditional craftsmanship into the modern digital era.

Another notable platform is **Fiverr (www.fiverr.com)**, which has revolutionized the way freelancers offer their services. Unlike traditional job websites, Fiverr flips the model by allowing freelancers to post gigs or services they can provide, starting at a nominal fee. This platform covers a broad spectrum of services, including graphic design, digital marketing, writing, video editing, and programming. Fiverr's unique approach provides freelancers with the flexibility to set their prices and terms, making it a versatile option for freelancers at different stages of their careers.

For those interested in selling their photography or designs, **Shutterstock (www.shutterstock.com)** and **Adobe Stock (stock.adobe.com)** provide platforms where creative content can be sold. Photographers, illustrators, and designers can upload their work to these sites, earning a commission each time their content is purchased for use. This model benefits creatives looking to earn passive income from their art without the need to handle physical products or manage a storefront.

Lastly, the digital marketplace is not limited to goods and creative services alone. Educational platforms like **Udemy (www.udemy.c om) and Coursera (www.coursera.org)** allow individuals to create and sell online courses on a wide range of subjects. These platforms have democratized education, enabling anyone with expertise in a particular field to share their knowledge with learners worldwide. It opens up avenues for professionals to earn by teaching about their areas of expertise, from programming languages to personal development courses.

The gig economy, therefore, encompasses a broad spectrum of opportunities, connecting skilled individuals with global audiences. By leveraging these online platforms, freelancers, creators, and educators can carve out successful careers, offering services and products that cater to the diverse needs of consumers worldwide.

Renting Out Assets: What You Need to Know

The concept of renting out personal assets has gained significant traction in the digital age, facilitated by platforms that seamlessly connect asset owners with interested renters. This segment of the gig economy allows individuals to monetize underused personal assets, ranging from real estate to vehicles, and even specialized equipment. Unlike traditional rental services, these digital platforms offer a peer-to-peer rental experience, which often results in more competitive pricing and a wider selection of unique offerings.

Platforms like **Airbnb (www.airbnb.com)** have revolutionized the way people travel and stay in different locations. By allowing individuals to rent out their homes, apartments, or even just a room, Airbnb has provided property owners a way to generate additional income while offering travelers more personalized and often less expensive accommodations than traditional hotels. Similarly, **VRBO (www.vrbo.com)** focuses on vacation rentals, providing options for larger groups wanting to stay together in a house or condo, offering home comforts along with the travel experience.

For those with vehicles that spend a lot of time sitting unused, **Turo (www.turo.com)** and **Getaround (www.getaround.com)** present opportunities to rent out personal vehicles to others. These services not only help car owners earn money from their parked vehicles but also provide a broader variety of car rental options to consumers, from daily errands to special occasions. This model benefits both the car owner and the renter, offering a personalized car rental experience not limited by the fleets and policies of traditional rental companies.

Lastly, for specialized equipment or other unique assets, platforms like **Fat Llama (www.fatllama.com)** allow individuals to rent almost anything to others in their local area. From cameras and drones to musical instruments and DJ equipment, Fat Llama connects those who need specific items for a short period with those willing to rent them out, fostering a community of sharing and making otherwise expensive items more accessible to those who need them temporarily. Through these platforms, the digital rental marketplace continues to grow, providing innovative ways for asset owners to monetize their possessions while offering renters diverse and affordable options.

Intellectual Property: Earning Royalties

In the realm of intellectual property, earning royalties represents a pivotal means through which creators can monetize their innovations or creative outputs. This model benefits authors, musicians, inventors, and various artists by allowing them to receive compensation every time their work is used or sold. Unlike the tangible assets shared through platforms like **Airbnb (www.airbnb.com)** or **Turo (www .turo.com)**, intellectual property deals with intangible assets, offering a different set of challenges and rewards.

Royalty agreements vary significantly across different industries. For example, in the publishing industry, authors typically earn royalties as a percentage of the sale price of their books. Major self-publishing platforms such as **Amazon's Kindle Direct Publishing (https ://kdp.amazon.com)** and **Barnes & Noble Press (www.barnesan dnoblepress.com)** offer accessible avenues for authors to publish their works and earn royalties, thus democratizing the access to publishing and selling literature.

In the music industry, the rise of streaming platforms like **Spotify (www.spotify.com)** and **Apple Music (www.music.apple.com)** has transformed how musicians earn royalties. These platforms pay artists a fraction of a cent each time someone streams their song, presenting both opportunities and challenges in building a financially sustainable career. Furthermore, licensing music for use in TV, movies, or advertising through sites like **Musicbed (www.musicbed.com)** or **Soundstripe (www.soundstripe.com)** can provide additional income streams for musicians and composers.

Lastly, for inventions, patents play a crucial role in protecting and monetizing innovations. Platforms such as **InventHelp (www.in venthelp.com)** provide inventors with the resources to patent their inventions and connect with companies interested in licensing or buying their patents. Earning royalties from patents requires a thorough understanding of the market and a strategic approach to protecting and licensing the invention. Across all these forms of intellectual property, the key to success lies in creating valuable, original content and effectively navigating the legal and commercial frameworks to monetize these assets.

Passive Income Strategies

Generative income streams from intellectual property offer vast opportunities but require an understanding of the platforms and strategic movements within these spheres. Among these, self-publishing is a significant revolution that has bypassed traditional gatekeepers of the publishing industry. Websites like **Amazon Kindle Direct Publishing (https://kdp.amazon.com)** and **Barnes & Noble Press (https://www.barnesandnoblepress.com)** provide authors with platforms to publish their works directly to a global audience. By taking advantage of these services, authors can maintain control over their content, pricing, and marketing strategies, thereby maximizing their potential royalties.

In the domain of music, the shift towards digital consumption has necessitated a new model for artists to earn a living from their craft. Streaming platforms such as **Spotify (https://www.spotify.com)** and **Apple Music (https://www.music.apple.com)** have become the forefront of music distribution. Although they offer artists global exposure, the challenge remains in navigating the relatively low pay-per-stream model. To supplement income, licensing platforms like **Musicbed (https://www.musicbed.com)** and **Soundstripe (https://www.soundstripe.com)** empower musicians to earn royalties through licensing their music for films, commercials, and other multimedia projects.

On the front of inventions and patents, securing and monetizing innovations is a nuanced process. **InventHelp (https://www.inve nthelp.com)** stands out as a valuable resource for inventors seeking to patent and market their inventions. The service not only aids in navigating the complex patent application process but also connects inventors with companies looking to license or acquire new innovations. Understanding the commercial viability and protecting the intellectual property rights of inventions is critical for success in this arena.

Success in monetizing intellectual property across these various platforms hinges on an in-depth understanding of the market, strategic content creation, and effective legal protection of assets. Authors, musicians, and inventors alike must continue to innovate and adapt to the rapidly changing landscape of digital content consumption. By leveraging these tools and platforms, creators can establish sustainable income streams and achieve greater financial independence through their intellectual property. The key lies in creating high-quality, original content and utilizing the right platforms to reach the intended audience.

Investments for Beginners

In the realm of investments, novices often find themselves bewildered by the variety of options and the complexities involved. Embarking on this financial journey necessitates a foundational understanding of different investment types, ranging from the stock market to real estate, and the varying degrees of risk associated with each. Websites like **Investopedia (https://www.investopedia.com)** serve as invaluable encyclopedias for all things investment-related, offering tutorials, definitions, and strategy advice to help beginners find their footing.

Another aspect crucial to the beginner investor's arsenal is the development of a diversified portfolio. Diversification is the practice of spreading investments across various financial instruments, industries, and other categories to reduce exposure to risk. The adage "don't put all your eggs in one basket" rings especially true in the investment world. Tools such as **Robinhood (https://www.robinhood.com)** and **Acorns (https://www.acorns.com)** can simplify this process for beginners, offering user-friendly platforms that guide users in making informed decisions about their investment spread.

Understanding the power of compound interest is a game-changer for those new to investing. Compound interest works by earning interest on the initial principal, which includes all of the accumulated interest from previous periods on a deposit or loan. This concept is beautifully illustrated by **Albert Einstein's** alleged quote calling compound interest the eighth wonder of the world. Calculators available on **Bankrate (https://www.bankrate.com)** allow individuals to visualize how their investments can grow over time, making it a practical resource for planning long-term financial goals.

Lastly, staying informed about market trends and financial news is crucial for making educated investment decisions. Websites like **Bloomberg (https://www.bloomberg.com)** and **The Wall Street Journal (https://www.wsj.com)** offer up-to-the-minute news, analysis, and commentaries that can impact investment strategies. By keeping abreast of global events and understanding their potential implications on markets, beginners can better anticipate shifts and adapt their investment portfolios accordingly.

Entering the investment world can be daunting, but with the right tools, information, and a cautious yet daring approach, beginners can lay down a path toward financial growth and security.

Networking for Freelance Opportunities

Building a robust network is crucial for freelancers seeking to expand their opportunities. In the digital age, numerous platforms exist to facilitate these connections, allowing freelancers to showcase their work, exchange ideas, and uncover new opportunities. Among them, **LinkedIn (https://www.linkedin.com)** stands out as a professional networking giant. Here, freelancers can connect with potential clients, participate in industry-specific groups, and share their portfolios, all of which can lead to fruitful collaborations and projects.

Another pivotal platform is **Upwork (https://www.upwork.com)**, a marketplace that bridges the gap between freelancers and businesses looking for specialized skills. By creating a detailed profile and bidding on projects that match their skills, freelancers can steadily build their portfolio and client base. Upwork's rating and review system also encourages transparency, allowing freelancers to build a reputable presence within the marketplace.

For creatives like writers, designers, and artists, **Behance (https://www.behance.net)** provides a visually oriented platform to display their work. Owned by Adobe, Behance allows creators to upload portfolios showcasing their projects, making it easier for potential clients and collaborators to discover their talents. Similarly, **Dribbble (https://www.dribbble.com)** offers a community for designers to share their work, receive feedback, and discover freelance opportunities.

Engaging in freelance communities is not just about seeking immediate job opportunities; it's also about building lasting relationships and a reputation in your field. Freelancers should actively participate in forums, attend webinars, and even consider contributing articles or thought leadership pieces to websites relevant to their expertise.

Medium (https://www.medium.com), for instance, is an excellent platform for publishing articles that reflect your knowledge and insights, potentially attracting the attention of clients needing your expertise. Starting is always the hardest part, but with persistence and the right strategy, freelancing can unfold into a rewarding career path.

Chapter Four

Maximizing Government Assistance and Tax Benefits

I n Chapter 4 of "The Hidden Money Manual: Find Cash to Pay
Your Bills Now," we turn our focus to an area often overlooked
but ripe with potential for improving your financial situation —
maximizing government assistance and tax benefits. Many individuals
and families are unaware of the numerous programs and incentives
available to them, which, if utilized correctly, can provide significant
financial support. This chapter aims to shed light on these resources,
guiding readers through the maze of eligibility requirements, application processes, and optimization strategies.

We will explore various forms of government assistance, from federal and state programs designed to aid those in need to more spe-

cialized grants and support services targeting specific groups such as veterans, seniors, and low-income families. Understanding these programs can make a substantial difference in one's financial health, offering relief in areas like housing, healthcare, education, and food security.

Additionally, we'll demystify the complex world of tax benefits, highlighting key deductions and credits that can lead to significant savings. From maximizing your retirement savings contributions to leveraging educational expenses and healthcare costs, this chapter aims to arm you with the knowledge to take full advantage of the tax code. Our goal is not just to help you find immediate financial relief but to set the foundation for long-term financial stability through smarter engagement with government resources and tax planning strategies.

Overview of Government Assistance Programs

Navigating the landscape of government assistance programs can initially seem daunting due to the sheer number of options and the specific eligibility criteria for each. However, understanding and accessing these resources can offer a lifeline for those struggling to make ends meet. Federal assistance programs such as the Supplemental Nutrition Assistance Program (SNAP), which provides food-purchasing assistance, and the Temporary Assistance for Needy Families (TANF), offering financial and medical aid to families, play crucial roles in supporting low-income individuals and families. Resources like serve as excellent starting points for exploring available federal assistance options, guiding users through a questionnaire to identify programs for which they might qualify.

On the state level, programs may vary significantly but often include subsidized healthcare through Medicaid, unemployment benefits, and various forms of housing assistance. These programs are designed to address the unique needs within each state, focusing on the most critical aspects of well-being for its residents. To explore state-specific assistance programs, visiting a state's official government website is recommended. For instance, offers detailed insights into healthcare benefits available across different states, providing vital information about eligibility and application processes.

Tax benefits, on the other hand, represent another avenue through which individuals can improve their financial situation. Many are unaware of the array of tax deductions and credits available, designed to reduce taxable income and, consequently, the amount of tax owed. Key examples include the Earned Income Tax Credit (EITC), designed for low to moderate-income earners, and the Child Tax Credit (CTC), which offers financial relief to families with children. The Internal Revenue Service (IRS) website, [IRS.gov](http://www.irs.gov), hosts a wealth of information on these and other tax benefits, including detailed guides on how to claim them.

Beyond these, there are numerous specialized grants and support services targeting veterans, seniors, students, and other specific groups. Organizations like the Department of Veterans Affairs () and the U.S. Department of Housing and Urban Development ([HUD.gov](http://www.hud.gov)) offer targeted assistance programs that cater to the distinct needs of these communities. For students, the Federal Student Aid website ([StudentAid.gov](http://www.studentaid.gov)) provides comprehensive information on grants, loans, and work-study programs available to aid in financing higher education.

Understanding and maximizing government assistance and tax benefits require time and effort but can significantly alleviate financial strain. By leveraging the resources and information provided by these websites, individuals and families can access the support they need, ensuring a more secure and stable financial future.

Navigating Benefits.gov

Maximizing benefits from government programs and assistance not only requires awareness but also a strategic approach to sifting through available resources. One of the primary steps towards effective utilization of government support is regularly checking official websites and platforms for updates and changes. Legislation, such as tax laws, can shift annually, affecting how individuals and families apply for and receive benefits. Sites like are crucial for keeping abreast of such changes, especially during tax season when new deductions or credits might be available.

Another critical aspect is understanding the eligibility criteria for various assistance programs. For instance, the Earned Income Tax Credit (EITC) has specific income thresholds that adjust each year. Similarly, the Child Tax Credit (CTC) and education-related benefits have their eligibility requirements. Websites like act as a gateway to explore a wide range of federal assistance programs, guiding users through eligibility questionnaires to identify programs that may offer them support.

For veterans and active military personnel, accessing specialized support services is crucial. The Department of Veterans Affairs website () provides comprehensive details on benefits such as healthcare, education, and housing specific to veterans. Additionally, the site offers tools for benefits navigation and application, making it an essential resource for veterans seeking to maximize their entitled support.

Lastly, it's important for borrowers and students to remain informed about changes in federal student aid, scholarships, and grants.

The Federal Student Aid website () is continually updated with the latest information on financial aid, application procedures, and deadlines. This site also includes resources for understanding the responsibilities that come with accepting federal aid, including loan repayment options and forgiveness programs.

In conclusion, while navigating the array of government assistance programs and tax benefits can appear daunting, leveraging official resources and websites can significantly simplify the process. By staying informed, understanding eligibility requirements, and systematically applying for relevant programs, individuals can harness these supports to enhance their financial wellbeing and security.

Applying for Unemployment Benefits Online

Navigating the complex landscape of unemployment benefits can be a daunting task for many individuals. Amidst job loss, understanding how to access these crucial supports can play a significant role in maintaining financial stability. The process starts with recognizing the official platforms where one can apply for unemployment benefits, ensuring that applications are submitted accurately and efficiently. Each state in the U.S. operates its own unemployment insurance program, which means the application process can vary significantly from one state to another.

To begin applying for unemployment benefits, individuals should first visit the website of their state's unemployment office. This can usually be done by conducting a simple internet search for "[State Name] unemployment benefits." For example, residents of New York would search for "New York State Department of Labor," leading them to , where they can find detailed information on how to apply for unemployment benefits, eligibility criteria, and the types of support available.

One key aspect of applying for unemployment benefits online is gathering all necessary documentation beforehand. This typically includes personal identification, employment history, and details regarding one's recent employment termination or reduction in hours. Preparing these documents in advance can streamline the application process, minimizing delays and potential errors. It's also crucial to review each state's specific requirements and guidelines to ensure a complete and accurate application.

After submitting an application, it's vital to stay informed about the status of your claim and respond promptly to any requests for additional information or clarification. Many states offer online portals where applicants can check their claim status, update personal information, and even file weekly claims once their application has been approved. Staying engaged with the process and utilizing available resources is essential for accessing the benefits designed to assist during times of unemployment.

In conclusion, while applying for unemployment benefits can initially seem overwhelming, leveraging the right resources and preparing accordingly can significantly ease the process. By visiting official state websites, gathering necessary documents ahead of time, and closely following application guidelines, individuals can access the support they need during challenging times.

SNAP Benefits: Eligibility and Application

Supplemental Nutrition Assistance Program (SNAP) benefits, formerly known as food stamps, provide essential support to millions of low-income individuals and families in the United States, helping

them afford nutritious food. The program is administered by the U
.S. Department of Agriculture (USDA), with eligibility requirements
and application processes varying slightly by state. This article outlines
the general guidelines for SNAP benefits eligibility, the application
process, and provides resources for further information.

Eligibility for SNAP Benefits

Eligibility for SNAP is primarily based on income, resources, and
household composition. Here are the key factors considered:

- **Income Limits**: Households must meet certain income limits, which are typically set at 130% of the Federal Poverty
  Level (FPL) for gross income and 100% of the FPL for net
  income, after deductions. These limits are adjusted annually
  and vary depending on household size.

- **Resources**: Assets or resources are also considered. Households without elderly (age 60 and over) or disabled members
  must have resources of $2,500 or less, while those with such
  members must have resources of $3,750 or less. Resources
  include cash, bank accounts, and other liquid assets but generally exclude a primary home, retirement savings, and most
  vehicles.

- **Work Requirements**: Able-bodied adults without dependents (ABAWDs) between the ages of 18 and 49 are required
  to work or participate in a work program for at least 80 hours
  per month to receive SNAP benefits beyond three months in
  a 36-month period, unless they are exempt.

- **Other Factors**: Citizenship status, residency, and household composition also play roles in determining eligibility.
  Generally, applicants must be U.S. citizens or hold certain

non-citizen statuses to qualify.

Application Process

The application process for SNAP benefits involves several steps:

- **Application Submission**: Applicants must fill out a state-specific SNAP application form, available through their state's SNAP agency. This form can typically be submitted online, by mail, or in person at a local SNAP office.

- **Documentation**: Applicants must provide documentation to verify their eligibility, including proof of income, expenses, residency, and identity. Required documents may vary by state.

- **Interview**: Most states require an interview with a SNAP caseworker, which can often be conducted over the phone. During the interview, the caseworker will review the application and documentation to determine eligibility.

- **Decision**: After the interview, the SNAP agency will send a notice of decision, usually within 30 days, indicating whether the application has been approved or denied and detailing the benefit amount if approved.

Accessing SNAP Benefits

If approved for SNAP, benefits are typically issued on an Electronic Benefit Transfer (EBT) card, which can be used like a debit card to purchase eligible food items at authorized retailers. The amount of SNAP benefits received depends on household size, income, and allowable deductions.

Resources for More Information

For the most accurate and detailed information regarding SNAP benefits, eligibility criteria, and the application process, it's important to consult resources specific to your state. Here are some general resources to get started:

- **USDA SNAP Website**: https://www.fns.usda.gov/snap/ supplemental-nutrition-assistance-program offers comprehensive information about the SNAP program, including eligibility requirements and links to state-specific SNAP information.

- **State SNAP Agencies**: Each state has its own SNAP agency website, which can be found through the USDA's SNAP State Directory of Resources at https://www.fns.usda.gov /snap/state-directory. These websites provide state-specific details on how to apply, office locations, and contact information.

- **SNAP Outreach Centers**: Many communities have SNAP outreach centers operated by non-profit organizations that can assist with the application process and answer questions about eligibility.

Remember, while the federal government sets the basic guidelines for SNAP, specific rules and processes can vary by state, so it's crucial to seek out the most current and relevant information directly from your state's SNAP agency or a trusted local resource.

Understanding Tax Credits and Deductions

While familiarizing yourself with SNAP benefits is a valuable step in managing your household's nutritional needs, it's equally important to understand another facet of financial health: tax credits and deductions. These elements of tax law can significantly impact your annual budget, potentially freeing up more funds for groceries, among other necessities. Understanding the different types of tax credits and deductions available can lead to substantial savings during tax time.

Tax credits are particularly beneficial because they reduce the amount of tax you owe, dollar for dollar. For instance, the Earned Income Tax Credit (EITC) is a refundable credit designed to benefit working individuals and families with low to moderate-income levels. Similarly, the Child Tax Credit can significantly decrease your tax liability if you have qualifying children. Both of these credits can increase your tax refund or reduce the amount you owe, thus enhancing your financial capabilities, including your ability to cover food expenses.

On the other hand, tax deductions lower your taxable income. They're based on expenses you've incurred during the tax year, such as charitable donations, mortgage interest, or certain work-related expenses. While deductions may not carry the immediate impact of tax credits, they can lower your overall taxable income, potentially dropping you into a lower tax bracket and reducing your overall tax obligation.

To maximize these tax advantages, it's crucial to keep meticulous records and receipts throughout the year. Consulting with a tax professional or utilizing reputable tax software can also ensure you're not overlooking any potential benefits. By strategically combining knowledge of federal assistance programs like SNAP with savvy tax planning, families can better manage their finances, ensuring more stability and security in meeting essential needs like nutrition and housing.

Free Tax Filing Services

In the digital age, free tax filing services have become increasingly accessible, providing individuals and families with the tools they need to manage their tax obligations efficiently and without additional costs. Websites like the IRS Free File (http://www.irs.gov/freefile) offer free tax preparation and filing services for taxpayers with income below a certain threshold. Eligible taxpayers can access software from leading tax preparation companies through this IRS-partnered program. This initiative not only simplifies the tax filing process but also ensures that you're taking full advantage of every tax credit and deduction you're entitled to.

Another valuable online resource is TurboTax Free Edition (http://www.turbotax.intuit.com/free-tax-filing). This service is tailored for taxpayers with simple tax returns, such as those without significant investments or rental properties. TurboTax guides users through each step of the filing process, offering clear explanations of tax laws and how they apply to your situation. By employing user-friendly interfaces and interactive help options, TurboTax makes it less daunting for individuals to file their taxes accurately and confidently.

For those seeking personalized tax assistance, the Volunteer Income Tax Assistance (VITA) program (http://www.irs.gov/Individuals/Free-Tax-Return-Preparation-for-You-by-Volunteers) is an excellent service. VITA provides free tax help to people who generally make $58,000 or less, persons with disabilities, and limited English-speaking taxpayers who need assistance in preparing their tax returns. IRS-certified volunteers offer this service in various community locations across the country, aiding in filing taxes correctly and maximizing potential refunds or minimizing liabilities.

Lastly, Credit Karma Tax (http://www.creditkarma.com/tax) offers a completely free tax filing service that covers a wide range of tax situations, from the simple to the more complex. It's a valuable resource for those seeking a no-cost solution that doesn't skimp on functionality. With a focus on maximizing refunds and ensuring accuracy, Credit Karma Tax verifies calculations and checks for potential errors before filing, providing peace of mind for users navigating the complexities of tax preparation.

By leveraging these free resources, taxpayers can demystify the tax filing process, ensure accuracy in their filings, and make informed decisions that bolster their financial health. The availability of these services marks a significant shift toward making tax preparation more accessible and less intimidating for all, paving the way for more individuals to maximize their returns and achieve greater financial stability.

Educational Grants and Scholarships

In today's increasingly expensive tertiary education landscape, educational grants and scholarships emerge as beacons of hope for many aspiring students. These financial aids are designed not just to alleviate the burden of tuition and other related expenses but also to empower students to achieve their academic and career goals without being weighed down by financial constraints. Unlike loans, grants and scholarships do not require repayment, making them highly sought after. Various organizations, including governmental bodies, educational institutions, and private entities, offer these awards based on criteria ranging from financial need and academic achievement to special talents and community service.

A comprehensive resource for finding scholarships is Scholarsh ips.com (http://www.scholarships.com). This platform offers a vast database of scholarships available across the United States, catering to a wide range of disciplines and specializations. By creating a free account, students can access personalized scholarship matches, making the search process more streamlined and efficient. Scholarships. com also provides valuable advice on how to apply for scholarships, writing winning essays, and avoiding scams, ensuring students are well-equipped to secure financial aid.

Another notable platform is Fastweb (http://www.fastweb.com), which has been connecting students to scholarships, grants, internships, and more for over 25 years. Fastweb's personalized matching system takes into account students' skills, interests, and career goals, presenting them with opportunities that best fit their profile. Furthermore, the site is rich with resources on college preparation, financial aid, career advice, and tips on how to maximize scholarship applications. Fastweb's commitment to delivering timely and relevant information makes it an indispensable tool for students navigating the complexities of funding their education.

The U.S. Department of Education's own Federal Student Aid website (http://www.studentaid.gov) is also an essential stop for anyone seeking financial assistance for higher education. It provides comprehensive information on federal grants, scholarships, and loans, including eligibility criteria, application processes, and deadlines. The site's FAFSA (Free Application for Federal Student Aid) section is particularly valuable, guiding students through the application process for federal financial aid—a critical step for anyone looking to secure educational grants and scholarships. By utilizing these resources, students can significantly enhance their chances of receiving financial support, ultimately paving the way for a brighter academic and professional future.

Housing Assistance Programs

In addition to scholarships and educational funding, housing assistance programs play a crucial role in supporting students' academic journeys, especially for those relocating for college or university. These programs aim to alleviate the financial burden of housing, ensuring students have a safe and stable environment conducive to learning. Among the numerous initiatives, university housing offices and external organizations offer various forms of aid, from subsidized housing to rental assistance schemes.

For students seeking on-campus housing solutions, most universities have dedicated housing offices that provide detailed information about dormitories and on-campus apartments. These departments assist with application processes, offer financial aid for housing, and sometimes even mediate conflicts or issues that arise. Students are encouraged to visit their university's housing website or contact the housing office directly to explore their options. Typically, university housing sites (e.g., `http://universityname.edu/housing`) offer a wealth of information, including application deadlines, costs, and eligibility criteria for financial assistance.

Off-campus housing assistance can be found through websites like Apartment Finder (`http://www.apartmentfinder.com`) and Rent Assistance (`http://www.rentassistance.us`). These platforms help students find affordable rental options near their institutions. Apartment Finder allows users to filter search results by price, location, and amenities, tailoring options to their specific needs. Rent Assistance, on the other hand, offers a directory of governmental and non-profit rental assistance programs, providing crucial support for students facing financial hardships.

Furthermore, for students looking for a more communal living experience, co-living spaces such as Common (`http://www.common.com`) offer flexible and affordable housing options in various cities.

These spaces are designed to promote community and shared experiences among residents, often including utilities and cleaning services in the rent. Co-living offers a unique alternative for students willing to share common areas while having a private bedroom, blending the lines between dormitory living and independent housing.

By leveraging these resources, students can find housing options that best suit their financial circumstances and personal preferences, enabling them to focus more on their studies and less on the stresses of securing affordable accommodation.

Veteran Benefits: A Guide

In navigating the complexities of securing affordable student housing, leveraging the right resources is pivotal. College and university housing offices are initial go-to points, offering exhaustive listings and advice tailored to students' needs. They often maintain comprehensive websites that detail housing options, both on-campus and off, complete with application deadlines, costs, and potential for financial assistance. Such resources prove invaluable, guiding students through the maze of accommodation choices.

For those students pivoting towards off-campus living, the digital realm offers a treasure trove of platforms dedicated to apartment hunting. Websites like Apartment Finder (`http://www.apartmentfinder.com`) and Rent Assistance (`http://www.rentassistance.us`) stand out for their comprehensive listings and user-friendly interfaces. Apartment Finder allows for a granular search based on various filters including price range, location, and even specific amenities, ensuring that students can find accommodations that meet their unique needs without the need to sift through irrelevant listings.

Rent Assistance, on the other hand, serves as a critical resource for students grappling with financial constraints. It offers an expansive directory of both government and non-profit rental assistance programs. This distinction is significant, providing a lifeline to students who may be facing financial hardships and are in dire need of support to secure stable housing. By bridging the gap between students and these essential services, Rent Assistance ensures that financial difficulties do not become a barrier to education.

Additionally, the rising popularity of co-living spaces opens up new avenues for students seeking affordable and sociable living arrangements. Platforms like Common (`http://www.common.com`) cater to this emerging need by offering co-living spaces in various cities. These setups promote a sense of community and shared experience among residents, striking a balance between privacy and communal living. With amenities often included in the rent, such as utilities and cleaning services, co-living spaces offer a compelling alternative for students wishing to blend the comfort of having a private bedroom with the vibrant social environment of shared living areas.

By optimizing these resources, students are better positioned to negotiate the challenges of finding suitable housing. From dedicated housing search platforms to co-living communities, the options are plentiful, ensuring that every student can find an accommodation strategy that aligns with their financial situation and personal preferences.

Childcare Assistance Resources

Juggling academic responsibilities with parenting duties presents a unique set of challenges for student-parents. Acknowledging this, numerous universities and community organizations have developed childcare assistance programs to support these individuals. These programs aim to alleviate some of the stresses associated with finding affordable and reliable childcare, enabling student-parents to focus more effectively on their studies. One prominent example is the Child Care Access Means Parents in School Program (CCAMPIS) funded by the U.S. Department of Education, which aids low-income student-parents in accessing quality childcare services.

Another valuable resource is the National Association for the Education of Young Children (NAEYC) website ('http://www.naeyc.org'), which provides a comprehensive directory of accredited childcare centers across the United States. This platform allows parents to search for facilities that meet rigorous quality standards, ensuring that their children are in a safe, nurturing environment. Additionally, NAEYC offers a variety of educational resources aimed at supporting both parents and educational professionals in the early childhood education sector.

Websites like Care.com ('http://www.care.com') also offer a platform for parents to find babysitters, nannies, and daycare options within their local area. This service allows users to filter potential caregivers based on a wide range of criteria, including experience, certifications, and reviews from other users. It's a valuable tool for student-parents who might have irregular schedules and need flexible childcare solutions that can accommodate their academic commitments.

Furthermore, some colleges and universities offer their own on-campus childcare facilities, specifically designed to cater to the needs of students and faculty. These centers often provide a sliding scale for fees based on income, making them an affordable option for many student-parents. Interested individuals should contact their institution's student services department to inquire about availabil-

ity and application procedures. Enhancing access to supportive resources such as childcare facilitates not only the academic success of
student-parents but also contributes positively to their mental and
emotional well-being, setting a foundation for a brighter future for
both parent and child.

Chapter Five

Leveraging Community and Non-Profit Organizations

In Chapter 5 of "The Hidden Money Manual," we pivot our focus towards the invaluable role that community and non-profit organizations play in our financial well-being. This chapter underscores the often-overlooked reality that resources and support are available within our own communities, ready to be tapped into by those in need. We explore how these organizations not only provide immediate assistance but also offer educational programs and tools for long-term financial empowerment. Whether you're facing a financial crisis, seeking educational opportunities, or in need of support services, local community and non-profit organizations can be a lifeline. This chapter aims to guide readers on how to effectively identify, engage with, and maximize the benefits from these resources. We'll cover the types of organizations that exist, the variety of services they offer, and tips on how to approach them for help. By weaving through the fabric of community solidarity, this chapter encourages readers to build networks of support that enhance financial stability and enrich lives beyond mere monetary measure.

Finding Local Food Banks and Pantries: A Guide to Accessing Emergency Food Assistance

In times of financial hardship, accessing nutritious food can become a challenge for many individuals and families. Local food banks and pantries play a crucial role in providing emergency food assistance to those in need, ensuring that no one has to go hungry. This article aims to guide you on how to find local food banks and pantries, understand what they offer, and prepare for your visit.

Understanding Food Banks and Pantries

Food Banks are large warehouse facilities that store and distribute tons of food to smaller hunger-relief agencies, including pantries, soup kitchens, and shelters. They typically receive food from various sources, including supermarkets, food manufacturers, and government programs.

Food Pantries operate as the arms that reach out to the community directly, providing free groceries on a one-time or recurring basis to individuals and families in need. They vary in size and operation but share the common goal of helping to alleviate hunger.

How to Find Local Food Banks and Pantries
   • **Feeding America's Food Bank Locator**

Website: http://www.feedingamerica.org/find-your-local-foodba nk

Feeding America is the nation's largest domestic hunger-relief organization. Their website features a Food Bank Locator tool where you can enter your zip code or state to find food banks in your area.

- **AmpleHarvest.org Pantry Finder**

Website: http://www.AmpleHarvest.org/find-pantry

AmpleHarvest.org connects gardeners with local pantries. Their Pantry Finder tool helps you locate participating food pantries to receive fresh produce and other food items.

- **211 Services**

Dial 211 or visit

211 is a free and confidential service that helps people find local resources, including food banks and pantries. You can call them or visit their website for assistance.

- **Local Government and Social Services**

Many local government offices and social service agencies maintain lists of food assistance resources. Check your city or county government's website for information.

- **Community Centers and Religious Organizations**

Local community centers, churches, mosques, synagogues, and other religious organizations often host food pantries or can direct you to nearby services.

Preparing for Your Visit

Before visiting a food pantry, it's helpful to:

- **Contact Ahead**: Verify operating hours, any ID or documentation needed, and if there are any specific eligibility requirements.

- **Bring Identification**: Some pantries may require proof of residency or income. It's wise to bring identification and any relevant documents.

- **Check for Special Programs**: Some pantries offer additional services or programs for children, the elderly, or those with dietary restrictions.

Tips for a Positive Experience
- **Be Respectful**: Remember that food banks and pantries are often staffed by volunteers doing their best to help.

- **Be Open**: Don't hesitate to accept different types of food. Pantries often provide a variety of items based on availability.

- **Give Back**: When you're able, consider donating food, time, or money to help others in your community.

Local food banks and pantries are lifelines for those facing food insecurity. By utilizing the resources mentioned above, individuals and families can find the support they need during difficult times. Remember, seeking help is a sign of strength, and contributing to these organizations when you can helps strengthen your community as a whole.

Utility Assistance Programs: Navigating Financial Support for Essential Services

As the cost of living continues to rise, many individuals and families find it increasingly difficult to cover basic utility costs such as electricity, gas, water, and telecommunications. Fortunately, there are numerous utility assistance programs available designed to help those struggling to pay their utility bills. This article will provide an overview of various types of utility assistance programs, how to find and apply for them, and additional tips for managing utility expenses.

Types of Utility Assistance Programs

- **Low-Income Home Energy Assistance Program (LI-HEAP)**

LIHEAP helps low-income households with their heating and cooling energy costs, bill payment assistance, energy crisis assistance, weatherization, and energy-related home repairs.

Website: http://www.acf.hhs.gov/ocs/programs/liheap

- **Weatherization Assistance Program (WAP)**

Provides low-income families with free weatherization services, such as improvements for heating and cooling systems, electrical upgrades, and insulation to help reduce energy bills.

Website: https://www.energy.gov/eere/wap/weatherization-assistance-program

- **Utility Company Assistance Programs**

Many utility companies offer their own assistance programs for customers facing financial difficulties. These can include payment plans, discounts for low-income customers, or emergency bill assistance.

- **State and Local Government Programs**

Various state and local government programs offer utility bill assistance, especially during extreme weather conditions. These programs may be specific to certain utilities like water or electricity.

- **Non-Profit and Charitable Organizations**

Organizations such as The Salvation Army, Catholic Charities, and community action agencies may offer emergency assistance with utility bills for those in need.

Finding Utility Assistance Programs

- **National Energy Assistance Referral (NEAR)**

NEAR is a free service that provides information about LIHEAP and other assistance programs.

Phone: 1-866-674-6327 or email: energyassistance@ncat.org

- **211 Services**

By dialing 211 or visiting , you can find local utility assistance programs as well as other essential community services.

- **State Department of Social Services**

Visit your state's department of social services website for information on available utility assistance programs and how to apply.

- **Utility Company Websites**

Check the website of your utility provider for information about any assistance programs they offer.

Applying for Utility Assistance Programs

- **Gather Necessary Documentation**: Before applying, you will likely need to provide proof of income, recent utility bills, and identification.

- **Apply Early**: Some programs have limited funding and serve on a first-come, first-served basis. Apply as soon as you anticipate needing assistance.

- **Seek Multiple Sources of Assistance**: Don't rely on a

single program. Explore various resources to maximize the support you can receive.

Tips for Managing Utility Bills

- **Energy Conservation**: Implement energy-saving measures at home, such as using energy-efficient appliances, sealing leaks, and adjusting thermostats.

- **Budget Billing**: Many utility companies offer budget billing plans that spread costs evenly throughout the year to avoid high bills during peak seasons.

- **Regular Monitoring**: Keep an eye on your utility usage to identify any unexpected increases that could indicate a leak or the need for maintenance.

Utility bills can be a significant burden for those struggling financially, but there are numerous assistance programs available to help. By taking advantage of these programs, individuals and families can find some relief from high utility costs. Remember, applying early and exploring multiple options can improve your chances of receiving assistance.

Non-Profit Credit Counseling Services: A Lifeline for Managing Debt

In the face of mounting debt, many individuals feel overwhelmed and uncertain about their financial future. Non-profit credit counseling services offer a beacon of hope, providing professional advice and structured plans to help people regain control of their finances. These organizations are dedicated to educating consumers, offering debt management programs, and guiding individuals towards financial stability without profit as their primary motive. This article will explore what non-profit credit counseling services are, the benefits they offer, how to find a reputable service, and what to expect during the process.

What Are Non-Profit Credit Counseling Services?

Non-profit credit counseling agencies are organizations that offer a range of services aimed at helping individuals manage their debt, improve their credit, and make informed financial decisions. These services typically include budget counseling, debt management plans (DMPs), financial education, bankruptcy counseling, and housing advice. Unlike for-profit debt settlement companies, non-profit credit counselors focus on education and long-term financial health.

Benefits of Using Non-Profit Credit Counseling Services

- **Comprehensive Financial Assessment**: Counselors provide a thorough review of your financial situation, including income, expenses, debts, and assets, to craft a personalized action plan.

- **Debt Management Plans (DMPs)**: If suitable, counselors can enroll you in a DMP, negotiating with creditors to lower interest rates, waive fees, and establish a repayment plan that consolidates multiple debts into a single monthly payment.

- **Financial Education and Resources**: These services often include workshops, seminars, and online resources to help you develop budgeting skills, understand credit reports, and make informed financial decisions.

- **Avoiding Bankruptcy**: For many, credit counseling can be a viable alternative to bankruptcy, helping to manage debt while maintaining a healthier credit score.

Finding Reputable Non-Profit Credit Counseling Services
- **National Foundation for Credit Counseling (NFCC)**

Website:

The NFCC is the largest and longest-serving nonprofit financial counseling organization in the United States. Its member agencies are accredited and adhere to high standards of excellence and transparency.

- **Financial Counseling Association of America (FCAA)**

Website:

The FCAA is another reputable organization that sets standards for quality credit counseling and debt management programs.

- **Check Accreditation and Certification**: Look for agencies that are accredited by the Council on Accreditation (COA) or another recognized body. Counselors should also be certified and trained in consumer credit, money and debt management, and budgeting.

- **Research and Reviews**: Look for reviews and testimonials from past clients, and check the Better Business Bureau (BBB) for any complaints.

What to Expect in the Credit Counseling Process
- **Initial Consultation**: Typically, the process begins with a free or low-cost consultation to assess your financial situation and discuss potential options.

- **Financial Education**: Counselors will work with you to understand the fundamentals of personal finance and how to manage your money more effectively.

- **Action Plan**: You'll receive a personalized plan to address your financial challenges, which may include enrolling in a DMP.

- **Ongoing Support**: Throughout the process, you'll have access to ongoing guidance and support from your counselor.

Non-profit credit counseling services can be a valuable resource for those struggling with debt, offering a pathway to financial stability without the high fees and potential scams associated with for-profit debt relief companies. By providing education, debt management plans, and personalized counseling, these organizations help individuals make informed decisions and take actionable steps towards a brighter financial future. Remember, the journey to debt freedom starts with reaching out for help, and non-profit credit counseling services are here to guide you every step of the way.

Community Education and Job Training Programs: Empowering Individuals for Career Success

Community education and job training programs serve as vital resources for individuals looking to enhance their skills, advance their careers, or transition into new job fields. These programs, often offered at local community colleges, vocational schools, non-profit organizations, and online platforms, are designed to meet the diverse needs of the community they serve. From acquiring new technical skills to improving literacy and numeracy, these programs play a crucial role in empowering individuals to achieve their career goals and contribute to the economic development of their communities. This article explores the types of programs available, their benefits, how to find them, and what participants can expect.

Types of Community Education and Job Training Programs

- **Vocational and Technical Training**: Offers hands-on training in specific trades such as automotive repair, healthcare, culinary arts, and information technology, preparing participants for direct entry into the workforce.

- **Adult Basic Education (ABE)**: Focuses on improving basic skills in reading, writing, and math for adults, often leading to a high school equivalency diploma.

- **English as a Second Language (ESL)**: Provides non-native speakers with language instruction to improve their reading, writing, speaking, and listening skills in English.

- **Workforce Development Programs**: Tailored to meet the needs of local employers, these programs offer training in skills that are in high demand in the local job market.

- **Professional Certification Courses**: Enable individuals to earn certifications in specific fields, enhancing their qualifications and job prospects.

Benefits of Participating in Community Education and Job Training Programs

- **Skill Enhancement**: Participants can acquire new skills or upgrade existing ones, making them more competitive in the job market.

- **Career Advancement**: These programs can lead to better job opportunities, higher salaries, and career progression.

- **Flexibility**: Many programs offer flexible schedules, including evening and weekend classes, to accommodate working adults.

- **Networking Opportunities**: Participants can connect with instructors, peers, and potential employers, expanding their professional network.

- **Affordability**: Compared to traditional four-year degree programs, community education and job training programs are often more affordable and offer financial aid options.

Finding Community Education and Job Training Programs

- **Local Community Colleges and Vocational Schools**: Check their websites or contact their admissions office for information on available programs.

- **Workforce Development Centers**: These centers offer career counseling, job training programs, and job placement services. Find your local center through the U.S. Department of Labor's website at https://www.careeronestop.org.

- **Public Libraries and Community Centers**: Often host or have information about educational workshops, seminars, and classes.

- **Online Platforms**: Websites like Coursera, edX, and Udacity offer a wide range of courses and professional certificate programs in collaboration with universities and companies.

What to Expect in Community Education and Job Training Programs

- **Assessment**: Many programs begin with an assessment to identify your skills, interests, and career goals.

- **Personalized Learning Plan**: Based on the assessment, a personalized plan is developed to address your specific educational and career objectives.

- **Instruction and Training**: Participants receive instruction from experienced professionals, with courses often combining classroom learning with hands-on training.

- **Support Services**: Many programs offer additional support services, including career counseling, resume writing workshops, and interview preparation.

- **Certification or Credential**: Upon completion, participants may receive a certificate, diploma, or professional credential, signaling their readiness to employers.

Community education and job training programs are invaluable resources for anyone looking to enhance their skills, change careers, or improve their employment prospects. By offering accessible, affordable, and flexible training options, these programs empower individuals to reach their full potential and contribute to the vitality of their communities. Whether you're a recent high school graduate, a working adult looking to advance your career, or someone seeking to pivot into a new industry, there's likely a program designed to meet your needs. Embracing the opportunities these programs provide can be the first step towards achieving your professional goals and securing a brighter future.

Medical and Dental Care Resources: Navigating Affordable Health Services

Access to affordable medical and dental care is a critical component of maintaining overall health and well-being. However, for many individuals and families, especially those without insurance or with limited coverage, finding cost-effective healthcare services can be challenging. Fortunately, a variety of resources are available to help bridge this gap, offering low-cost or free medical and dental care to those in need. This article explores the types of available healthcare resources, their benefits, how to find them, and what individuals can expect when seeking out these services.

Types of Medical and Dental Care Resources

- **Community Health Centers**: Federally-funded health centers provide primary care services on a sliding fee scale based on income, making healthcare accessible to underserved communities.

- **Free Clinics**: Operated by volunteer health professionals, free clinics offer a range of medical services at no cost, focusing on uninsured and low-income individuals.

- **Dental Schools and Hygiene Programs**: Many dental schools and hygiene programs offer low-cost dental services to the public as a way for their students to gain practical experience under professional supervision.

- **State Health Departments**: Provide various public health services, including immunizations, screenings, and sometimes dental care, often at reduced costs or for free.

- **Non-Profit Organizations**: Organizations such as the HealthWell Foundation and the Patient Access Network Foundation offer financial assistance and resources for specific health care needs and conditions.

Benefits of Utilizing These Resources

- **Cost Savings**: Accessing these services can significantly reduce medical and dental expenses, especially for routine care, preventative services, and early treatment.

- **Improved Health Outcomes**: Regular access to healthcare services leads to better disease management, improved health outcomes, and a reduction in emergency room visits and hospitalizations.

- **Comprehensive Care**: Many community health centers and clinics provide comprehensive services, including primary care, dental care, mental health services, and pharmacy services, ensuring holistic care.

- **Community Support**: These resources often offer additional support services, such as health education, nutritional counseling, and social services, contributing to overall well-being.

Finding Medical and Dental Care Resources

- **Health Resources and Services Administration (HRSA)**

    a. Website: https://findahealthcenter.hrsa.gov

    b. HRSA's website helps users locate federally-funded health centers that provide services based on your ability to pay.

- **Dental Schools Directory**

    a. Conduct an internet search for dental schools or dental hygiene programs in your area. These institutions often have clinics that offer public services.

- **State and Local Health Departments**

    a. Visit the website of your state or local health department for information on public health clinics and services.

- **FreeClinics.com**

    a. Website: https://www.freeclinics.com

    b. A resource for finding free and low-cost clinics offering medical and dental care across the United States.

- **Non-Profit Organizations and Charities**

    a. Organizations such as the United Way (dial 211) can provide referrals to local health services and resources.

What to Expect When Seeking Care
- **Eligibility Verification**: You may need to provide income information or proof of insurance status to qualify for sliding scale fees or free services.

- **Appointments**: Some clinics operate on a walk-in basis, while others require appointments. It's advisable to call ahead to understand the clinic's policies.

- **Documentation**: Bring any medical or dental records you have, a list of medications, and identification.

- **Quality Care**: Despite the reduced cost, the care provided by these resources is often on par with standard medical and dental practices, as many professionals volunteering or working in these settings are highly qualified and dedicated to public service.

Navigating the landscape of affordable medical and dental care resources can dramatically improve access to essential health services for uninsured and underinsured individuals. By taking advantage of community health centers, free clinics, dental school programs, and state health services, individuals can receive the care they need without the burden of excessive costs. Remember, preventive care and early treatment are key to maintaining long-term health and avoiding more serious, costly medical issues down the line. Utilizing these resources not only benefits individual health but also supports the broader goal of enhancing public health and well-being.

Legal Aid Services for Financial Issues: Navigating Legal Challenges with Professional Support

Legal challenges can be daunting, especially when they pertain to financial issues such as debt, bankruptcy, consumer rights, and housing. For individuals facing financial hardships, the cost of legal representation might seem prohibitive. Fortunately, legal aid services exist to provide free or low-cost legal assistance to those in need, helping them navigate the complexities of the legal system and protect their financial interests. This article will discuss the types of legal aid services available for financial issues, the benefits of using these services, how to find them, and what to expect during the process.

Types of Legal Aid Services for Financial Issues

- **Debt and Bankruptcy Assistance**: Offers guidance and representation for dealing with creditors, negotiating debt settlements, and filing for bankruptcy.

- **Consumer Protection**: Provides legal assistance for issues related to consumer rights, including disputes with service providers, fraudulent practices, and warranty issues.

- **Foreclosure and Housing**: Helps homeowners facing foreclosure to understand their rights and options, and assists renters with issues such as evictions and landlord disputes.

- **Tax Disputes**: Offers assistance with disputes related to federal, state, and local taxes, including representation in front of the IRS or state tax agencies.

- **Public Benefits Advocacy**: Assists individuals in applying for, appealing, and maintaining eligibility for public benefits such as Social Security, Medicaid, and food stamps.

Benefits of Using Legal Aid Services

- **Access to Justice**: Legal aid services ensure that financial constraints do not prevent individuals from receiving fair legal representation.

- **Expert Guidance**: Beneficiaries receive advice and representation from experienced attorneys who are knowledgeable about financial laws and regulations.

- **Cost Savings**: These services are provided free or at a low cost, significantly reducing the financial burden of legal proceedings.

- **Stress Reduction**: Navigating legal challenges with professional support can alleviate stress and anxiety associated with financial legal issues.

Finding Legal Aid Services for Financial Issues

- **Legal Services Corporation (LSC)**

  a. Website: https://www.lsc.gov

  b. The LSC is an independent nonprofit established by Congress to provide financial support for civil legal aid to low-income Americans. The website features a search tool to find local legal aid organizations.

- **National Consumer Law Center (NCLC)**

  a. Website: https://www.nclc.org

  b. The NCLC provides extensive resources on consumer advocacy and legal issues, including guides on finding legal assistance.

- **American Bar Association (ABA)**

  a. Website: https://www.americanbar.org/groups/legal_services/flh-home

  b. The ABA's Free Legal Answers program offers a virtual legal clinic where users can ask questions and receive answers from pro bono lawyers.

- **State and Local Bar Associations**

  a. Many state and local bar associations offer referral services to connect individuals with legal aid organizations or pro bono attorneys.

- **Law School Clinics**

  a. Law schools often operate clinics where law students, supervised by faculty members, provide legal services for free. Check with local law schools for available services.

What to Expect in the Legal Aid Process

- **Eligibility Screening**: Most legal aid organizations require an initial screening to determine eligibility based on income and the nature of the legal issue.

- **Consultation**: Eligible individuals are typically offered a consultation with a legal professional to discuss their case and explore options.

- **Representation**: Depending on the case and available resources, the legal aid organization may offer direct representation or refer the individual to a pro bono attorney.

- **Educational Resources**: Many organizations also provide workshops, seminars, and online resources to educate individuals about their legal rights and responsibilities.

Legal aid services play a critical role in ensuring that financial issues do not lead to unjust outcomes for those unable to afford private legal representation. By providing access to expert guidance, representation, and educational resources, legal aid organizations empower individuals to address their financial legal challenges with confidence. If you're facing a financial legal issue, consider reaching out to a legal aid service for support. Remember, the first step towards resolving legal challenges is seeking professional assistance, and legal aid services are here to help.

Accepting Donations During Hard Times: A Guide to Navigating Support Networks

In periods of financial hardship or personal crisis, accepting donations can provide much-needed relief and support. Many individuals and families find themselves in situations where external help becomes necessary to navigate through tough times. This guide aims to highlight how to gracefully accept donations, the types of donations available, and where to find assistance, including websites and resources that can connect you with the help you need.

Types of Donations Available

- **Monetary Donations**: Cash donations are often the most flexible form of assistance, allowing you to address your most pressing needs directly.

- **Food Assistance**: Donations of food can come from food banks, pantries, or community drives, helping to alleviate grocery expenses.

- **Clothing and Household Goods**: Donations of new or gently used clothing, furniture, and other household essentials can be crucial for those who have lost belongings or cannot afford to buy these items.

- **Professional Services**: Some organizations and individuals offer free professional services, such as legal aid, medical care, or career counseling, to those in need.

Websites and Resources for Finding Assistance
- **GoFundMe**: https://www.gofundme.com

   a. A crowdfunding platform that allows individuals to create fundraising campaigns for personal causes, including financial hardship, medical bills, and more.

- **Feeding America**: http://www.feedingamerica.org

   a. The nation's largest domestic hunger-relief organization, with a network of 200 food banks and 60,000 food pantries and meal programs across the country.

- **Goodwill**: https://www.goodwill.org

   a. Offers clothing and household goods to those in need through its retail stores and donation centers.

- **Salvation Army**: https://www.salvationarmyusa.org

   a. Provides a wide range of assistance, including food, clothing, shelter, and counseling services.

- **211**: http://www.211.org

   a. Connects people with local resources for food, housing, utility assistance, emergency help, and more. Simply dial 211 to reach assistance in your area.

How to Accept Donations
- **Be Open and Honest**: Transparency about your situation

and needs can help build trust with potential donors.

- **Utilize Social Media and Online Platforms**: Sharing your story on social media or platforms like GoFundMe can widen your reach.

- **Connect with Local Charities and Non-profits**: Many organizations are dedicated to providing specific types of assistance. Reaching out directly can connect you with resources tailored to your needs.

- **Thank the Donors**: Whether through a personal message, social media post, or thank-you note, expressing gratitude is important.

Managing Donations

- **Prioritize Your Needs**: Use monetary donations for the most urgent bills or needs first, such as housing, utilities, or medical expenses.

- **Budget Wisely**: If you receive a substantial amount, consider creating a budget to stretch the funds as far as possible.

- **Seek Financial Counseling**: Some organizations offer free financial counseling to help you manage donations and plan for the future.

Accepting donations during hard times can significantly alleviate stress and provide the means to get back on your feet. By leveraging the resources available online and in your community, you can find the support you need. Remember, it's okay to ask for help, and there are many people and organizations willing to support you. Whether it's through monetary assistance, food, clothing, or professional services, accepting donations can be a vital step toward stability and recovery.

Support Groups for Financial Stress: Finding Community and Coping Strategies

Financial stress can be an overwhelming experience, impacting mental health and overall well-being. Fortunately, support groups exist to provide a space for individuals to share their experiences, offer mutual support, and learn coping strategies. These groups, whether in-person or online, can be a valuable resource for navigating the challenges associated with financial hardship. This article will explore the types of support groups available for financial stress, the benefits of participating, how to find these groups, and what to expect when joining.

Types of Support Groups for Financial Stress

- **Debtors Anonymous (DA)**: A 12-step program for those struggling with debt and financial difficulties, offering a path to solvency through mutual support and shared experiences.

    a. Website: https://debtorsanonymous.org

- **Personal Finance Support Groups**: These groups focus on budgeting, saving, investing, and other aspects of personal finance, providing a space to learn and grow financially.

    a. Example Platform: Reddit's r/personalfinance community offers advice and support on a wide range of financial topics.

    b. Website: https://www.reddit.com/r/personalfinance/

- **Financial Therapy Association (FTA)**: While not a support group per se, FTA connects individuals with financial therapists who offer support for emotional and psychological aspects of financial stress.

    a. Website: https://www.financialtherapyassociation.org

- **Online Forums and Social Media Groups**: Platforms like Facebook and online forums host various groups where individuals can share experiences, advice, and support regarding financial stress.

Benefits of Participating in Support Groups for Financial Stress

- **Shared Experiences**: Meeting others who are facing similar financial challenges can provide comfort and reduce feelings of isolation.

- **Practical Advice**: Members often share practical tips and resources that have helped them manage their finances better.

- **Emotional Support**: These groups offer a safe space to express feelings and concerns related to financial stress, promoting emotional well-being.

- **Accountability**: Many find that participating in support groups helps them stay accountable to their financial goals.

Finding Support Groups for Financial Stress

- **Search Online**: Websites like Meetup (https://www.meetup.com) often list local and virtual support groups for a variety of issues, including financial stress.

- **Ask Financial Counselors**: Financial counselors or advisors may know of local support groups or resources in the community.

- **Check Community Centers**: Local community centers, libraries, or religious organizations often host or can direct you to support groups.

- **Explore Social Media**: Search platforms like Facebook for groups dedicated to financial well-being and stress relief.

What to Expect When Joining a Support Group

- **Introductions**: Initially, you might be asked to share your story or why you sought out the group, but sharing is typically voluntary.

- **Confidentiality**: Members are usually asked to agree to confidentiality terms, ensuring a safe and private environment.

- **Regular Meetings**: Many groups meet regularly, whether weekly or monthly, providing consistent support.

- **Diverse Perspectives**: Expect to encounter members at various stages of their financial journey, offering a range of insights and experiences.

Support groups for financial stress offer a unique combination of emotional support, practical advice, and a sense of community that can be incredibly helpful during tough financial times. Whether you're dealing with debt, budgeting challenges, or the emotional toll of financial insecurity, there's likely a group that fits your needs. By reaching out and connecting with others who understand what you're going through, you can find not just support, but also hope and strategies for a more secure financial future.

Volunteer Opportunities for Skill Building: Enhancing Your Career Through Service

Volunteering is not only a noble way to give back to your community but also a powerful tool for personal and professional development. Many individuals leverage volunteer opportunities to build skills, gain experience, and enhance their resumes, particularly in fields where practical experience is as valuable as formal education. This article explores various volunteer opportunities for skill-building, the benefits of these experiences, how to find them, and what to expect from your volunteer journey.

Types of Volunteer Opportunities for Skill Building

- **Non-Profit Organizations**: Engage in roles ranging from administrative tasks to direct service provision, ideal for developing organizational, leadership, and interpersonal skills.

    a. Example: VolunteerMatch (https://www.volunteerma tch.org) connects volunteers with non-profit organizations based on interest and skill area.

- **Professional Associations**: Many associations offer volunteer positions on committees or boards, which can be perfect for networking and developing professional skills relevant to your career field.

    a. Example: Taproot Foundation (https://www.taprootf oundation.org) facilitates connections between professionals and non-profits for pro bono consulting projects.

- **Educational Tutoring and Mentoring**: Volunteering as a tutor or mentor can help develop teaching, mentoring, and communication skills while making a difference in the lives of students or young professionals.

    a. Example: Tutor.com (https://www.tutor.com) offers opportunities to tutor students in various subjects online.

- **International Volunteering**: Offers a chance to develop cross-cultural communication, adaptability, and foreign language skills, among others, in an international setting.

    a. Example: Peace Corps (https://www.peacecorps.gov) provides opportunities for extended volunteer service abroad with comprehensive training and support.

- **Emergency and Disaster Relief**: Volunteering with organizations that provide emergency services can help develop skills in crisis management, emergency planning, and first aid.

    a. Example: The Red Cross (https://www.redcross.org) offers a wide range of volunteer opportunities in disaster relief, health and safety training, and more.

Benefits of Volunteering for Skill Building

- **Hands-On Experience**: Volunteering provides practical experience that can be invaluable for career development or transitioning into a new field.

- **Networking Opportunities**: Connect with professionals in your field of interest who can provide mentorship, references, and job leads.

- **Skill Diversification**: Develop a broad range of transferable skills, from technical skills specific to your field to soft skills like teamwork and problem-solving.

- **Personal Growth**: Gain a sense of accomplishment, improve self-esteem, and develop empathy by contributing to your community.

Finding Volunteer Opportunities for Skill Building

- **Online Volunteer Platforms**: Websites like Idealist (https://www.idealist.org) and VolunteerMatch offer searchable databases of volunteer opportunities based on skill set, interests, and location.

- **Local Community Centers and Libraries**: Often have information on local volunteer opportunities and may host volunteer fairs.

- **University and College Career Centers**: Provide resources for students and alumni to connect with volunteer opportunities that can enhance their career prospects.

- **Social Media and Professional Networking Sites**: LinkedIn's Volunteer Marketplace (https://www.linkedin.com) allows users to find volunteer opportunities that match their professional skills and goals.

What to Expect When Volunteering

- **Orientation and Training**: Most organizations provide some form of orientation or training to prepare you for your volunteer role.

- **Commitment**: Some positions may require a minimum time commitment or specific hours, so it's important to choose opportunities that fit your schedule.

- **Supervision and Support**: You'll likely be assigned a supervisor or mentor to guide you through your volunteer experience and help you maximize your skill development.

- **Evaluation and Feedback**: Many organizations offer evaluations or feedback sessions to help volunteers grow and improve in their roles.

Volunteering offers a unique and rewarding pathway to skill development, providing tangible benefits for career advancement while contributing positively to society. By carefully selecting opportunities aligned with your career goals and personal values, you can gain invaluable experience, expand your professional network, and enhance your resume. Whether your interests lie in non-profit work, education, international service, or emergency relief, there's a volunteer opportunity out there for you to build skills and make a difference.

Community-Supported Agriculture (CSA) Programs: Connecting Consumers with Local Farms

Community-Supported Agriculture (CSA) programs offer a unique model for buying local, seasonal food directly from a farmer. Through these programs, consumers can purchase a "share" of a farm's harvest and receive regular distributions of fresh produce and other farm products. CSAs foster a closer connection between consumers and their food sources, support local agriculture, and promote sustainable farming practices. This article will explore the workings of CSA programs, their benefits, how to find one near you, and what to expect as a CSA member.

What are CSA Programs?

CSA programs involve a partnership between a farm and a community of consumers. Members pay in advance for a season's worth of agricultural products, which in turn provides the farm with early-season capital. Throughout the growing season, members receive weekly or bi-weekly shares of the farm's harvest, typically consisting of vegetables and fruits, and possibly including eggs, meat, dairy products, and baked goods, depending on the farm.

Benefits of Joining a CSA Program

- **Fresh, Seasonal Produce**: Enjoy the freshest possible produce, often picked the same day it's delivered to you.

- **Support Local Farmers**: Your membership helps provide financial stability to local farmers, allowing them to focus on sustainable farming practices.

- **Environmental Sustainability**: CSAs often use organic or low-impact farming methods, reducing the environmental footprint of agriculture.

- **Discover New Foods**: Being part of a CSA encourages trying new vegetables and fruits and learning how to cook them.

- **Community Connection**: Many CSAs offer farm visits, events, and volunteer opportunities, fostering a sense of community among members and farmers.

Finding CSA Programs Near You

- **Local Harvest**

a. Website: https://www.localharvest.org/csa/

b. Local Harvest provides a comprehensive directory of CSA programs across the United States, making it easy to find one near you.

- **USDA National Farmers Market Directory**

  a. Website: https://www.ams.usda.gov/local-food-direct ories/farmersmarkets

  b. While primarily a directory for farmers markets, this USDA resource can also help you connect with local farmers who may offer CSA shares.

- **Agricultural Cooperative Extension Offices**

  a. Your local cooperative extension office can provide information about CSAs and other direct-to-consumer farm programs in your area.

- **Farmers Markets and Local Food Co-ops**

  a. Visiting a farmers market or local food co-op can lead to direct connections with farmers who offer CSA programs.

What to Expect as a CSA Member

- **Seasonal Eating**: CSA shares reflect the growing season, so the variety and quantity of produce will change throughout the year.

- **Shared Risk**: Members share in the risks of farming, including poor harvests due to unfavorable weather conditions or pests.

- **Payment and Pickup**: Members typically pay for the season upfront, though some CSAs offer payment plans. You'll pick up your share at a designated location weekly or bi-weekly.

- **Community Involvement**: Many CSAs encourage members to visit the farm, participate in workdays, and attend events.

Joining a Community-Supported Agriculture (CSA) program is a rewarding way to support local farmers, eat fresh and seasonal food, and become part of a community committed to sustainable agriculture. By investing in a share of a farm's harvest, you're not only ensuring a supply of fresh produce for yourself and your family but also contributing to the health of your local economy and environment. Explore the resources listed above to find a CSA program near you and experience the benefits of fresh, farm-to-table eating.

Chapter Six

Navigating Financial Products and Services

I n Chapter 6 of "The Hidden Money Manual: Find Cash to Pay Your Bills Now," we venture into the complex world of financial products and services, a territory vast and varied, often daunting to the average consumer. This chapter is designed to serve as a comprehensive guide, demystifying the complexities that surround financial instruments and services. Whether it's navigating the intricacies of bank accounts, understanding the nuances of various investment vehicles, or choosing the right insurance policies, our objective is to empower you with the knowledge necessary to make informed decisions.

As we explore the landscape of financial products, we'll dissect how each can play a pivotal role in your broader financial strategy. The aim is not only to acquaint you with the range of options available but also to highlight how to effectively evaluate and utilize these tools to bolster your financial health. From the fundamental basics of checking and savings accounts to the more complex realms of stocks, bonds, and mutual funds, we'll provide clear explanations and actionable advice.

Furthermore, this chapter will address the vital importance of choosing financial services that align with your personal goals and values. With the financial market's constant evolution and the introduction of new technology-driven services, it's crucial to stay informed and adaptable. We'll guide you through assessing the reliability, costs, and benefits of traditional vs. digital banking, investment services, and insurance offerings.

By the end of this chapter, you will possess a deeper understanding of financial products and services, equipping you with the confidence to navigate the financial world more adeptly. Armed with this knowledge, you'll be better positioned to craft a financial plan that not only addresses your immediate needs but also lays a solid foundation for long-term financial stability and growth.

Comparing Loan Options: Interest Rates and Terms

When venturing into the domain of loans, understanding and comparing interest rates and terms between different options becomes paramount. Interest rates, the cost of borrowing money, can significantly affect the total amount you'll end up repaying. Loans can have fixed rates, where the interest stays constant over the life of the loan, or variable rates, which can fluctuate with market changes. Deciphering these nuances allows borrowers to foresee and manage their repayment strategy effectively.

Equally critical to consider are the terms of a loan, which outline the repayment period, frequency of payments, and any possible penalties for early repayment or defaults. Short-term loans might offer higher monthly payments but lower total interest over the loan's life, whereas long-term loans can ease the monthly financial burden at the cost of higher overall interest. Each borrower's situation will dictate which loan term is most suitable, emphasizing the necessity of a thorough comparison based on personal financial status and goals.

Furthermore, potential borrowers should investigate additional fees and costs associated with loans, such as origination fees, application fees, and any penalties. These can add up and significantly impact the affordability and appeal of certain loan options over others. Transparency about all associated costs from the outset is crucial in making an informed choice.

Lastly, while comparing loan options, it's essential to utilize reputable sources and tools for information. Many financial institutions and independent financial advice websites offer loan comparison tools and calculators, which can help simplify this complex process. Although I can't list specific URLs, most major banking websites and financial advice platforms typically have such resources. Always ensure you're using secure and reliable sites for your financial research to avoid misinformation and potential fraud. Conducting thorough research and comparisons will steer you towards making a loan choice that aligns with your financial objectives and capabilities, paving the way for a more secure financial future.

Understanding Credit Card Offers

Understanding credit card offers is another crucial aspect of personal finance, mirroring the complexities and considerations involved in loan comparisons. Credit cards are not just means of accessing unsecured credit; they can also be tools for building credit history, earning rewards, and managing finances if used responsibly. However, the wide array of credit card offers available makes it essential for potential cardholders to scrutinize various factors before making a choice.

Firstly, interest rates, or Annual Percentage Rates (APR), demand attention. Credit cards typically come with different APRs for purchases, cash advances, and balance transfers. A card with a low introductory APR might be appealing, but it's important to understand how long the introductory period lasts and what the rate will increase to afterward. This is particularly significant if you anticipate carrying a balance on the card.

Rewards and benefits are another key consideration. Many credit cards offer rewards such as cash back, points, or miles based on the amount of spending. Some cards are tailored to specific expenditures like travel, dining, or groceries, offering higher rewards rates in these categories. Beyond rewards, cards might also offer perks such as travel insurance, extended warranties on purchases, and concierge services. Weighing these rewards and benefits against any annual fees is crucial to determining the card's overall value.

Lastly, it's important to factor in the credit card's fees and penalties. These can include annual fees, late payment fees, foreign transaction fees, and more. Additionally, understanding the grace period—a period during which you can pay your balance in full to avoid interest charges—is essential. Reading the fine print and understanding all associated costs and terms will help in selecting a credit card that aligns with your spending habits and financial goals, ultimately achieving a positive impact on your financial health and credit score.

The Pros and Cons of Refinancing

Refinancing a mortgage is a strategic financial decision that homeowners might consider for various reasons, including the desire to take advantage of lower interest rates, reduce monthly mortgage payments, or change the term of the loan. Lowering the interest rate, even by a small percentage, can result in significant savings over the life of the loan. However, this process also incurs closing costs and fees, which can range from 2% to 6% of the loan's principal. It's essential to calculate whether the potential savings from refinancing outweigh these upfront costs.

Another aspect to consider is the opportunity to switch from an adjustable-rate mortgage (ARM) to a fixed-rate mortgage, or vice versa. Homeowners might prefer the stability of fixed-rate mortgages, which provide predictable monthly payments. Conversely, an ARM may offer lower initial rates, which could be advantageous for those planning to move or refinance again within a few years. The choice depends on the homeowner's financial situation, goals, and market conditions.

Refinancing can also serve as a tool for debt consolidation, allowing homeowners to convert higher-interest debt into a lower-interest mortgage loan. This can simplify finances by consolidating multiple payments into a single, more manageable monthly payment. However, turning unsecured debt into secured debt could pose risks, such as the potential loss of the home if payments cannot be maintained. It's critical to assess one's financial stability and long-term ability to meet the new mortgage obligations.

Lastly, the decision to refinance should factor in the homeowner's future plans. Staying in the home long enough to reach the "break-even point"—where the savings from the lower interest rate exceed the costs of refinancing—is necessary to justify the decision. Refinancing offers significant benefits but also requires careful consideration of one's financial goals, the current and projected interest rate environment, and personal circumstances. Consulting with a financial advisor can help homeowners make a well-informed decision that aligns with their long-term financial plans.

Hardship Withdrawal Options from Retirement Accounts

In light of financial emergencies or unexpected expenses, many individuals consider taking hardship withdrawals from their retirement accounts as a last-resort solution. These withdrawals allow account holders to access funds before retirement age, often to cover immediate, significant expenses such as medical bills, tuition fees, or preventing home foreclosure. However, while such withdrawals can provide necessary relief in dire situations, they come with substantial considerations and potential repercussions.

Firstly, it's crucial to understand the tax implications associated with hardship withdrawals. Typically, any funds withdrawn from retirement accounts like a 401(k) or an IRA before reaching the age of 59 ½ are subject to both income tax and a 10% early withdrawal penalty. This can significantly reduce the amount received by the account holder, making it less beneficial than initially thought. Some exceptions exist, such as specific medical expenses or a first-time home purchase, but the general rule makes these withdrawals costly.

Additionally, hardship withdrawals can have long-term effects on retirement savings. Withdrawing funds prematurely interrupts the compound interest process, potentially resulting in a substantial reduction in future retirement savings. This is particularly concerning given the uncertainties of social security benefits and the increasing life expectancy, which demand more substantial personal retirement savings than ever before.

It's also worth noting that not all retirement accounts offer the option for hardship withdrawals, and those that do often have strict rules regarding eligibility and documentation. Employers and account custodians typically require proof of immediate and heavy financial need, as defined by the IRS. Given these restrictions, individuals should explore all other financial avenues, such as loans or payment plans, before resorting to a hardship withdrawal.

In conclusion, while hardship withdrawals can provide necessary funds during financial crises, the long-term consequences and costs associated with them make it essential for individuals to consider all options and consult with a financial advisor. Planning for emergencies by building a liquid savings fund can also help mitigate the need for such measures.

Emergency Fund Accounts: Where to Keep Your Money

Deciding where to keep your emergency fund is crucial for ensuring its accessibility and growth, while also keeping it separate from your day-to-day spending accounts. A high-yield savings account is often the most recommended option. These accounts offer higher interest rates than standard savings accounts, meaning your emergency fund will grow while it sits, albeit at a rate typically below inflation. Importantly, high-yield savings accounts are liquid, ensuring that funds can be withdrawn without penalties or delays when an emergency arises. Additionally, these accounts are insured by the Federal Deposit Insurance Corporation (FDIC) up to $250,000, providing a layer of security for your savings.

Another option is a money market account, which combines features of both savings and checking accounts. Money market accounts typically offer higher interest rates than regular savings accounts and come with the ability to write checks or use a debit card, increasing the accessibility of funds. However, like high-yield savings accounts, they are also subject to federal regulations that limit the number of certain types of withdrawals or transfers each month, so it's vital to understand these restrictions before choosing this option for your emergency fund.

Certificates of Deposit (CDs) can also be considered for a portion of an emergency fund, especially the amount that is not immediately needed. CDs generally offer higher interest rates than savings accounts in exchange for locking in your funds for a predetermined period. The downside is the lack of flexibility, as early withdrawal of funds from a CD usually incurs a penalty which can negate the interest earned. A possible strategy is the CD ladder, where multiple CDs with staggered maturity dates provide a balance between accessibility and maximizing interest earnings.

Lastly, for those with a high-risk tolerance, considering a portion of the emergency fund in a conservative investment portfolio may be an option. This could potentially yield higher returns but comes with the risk of loss and should only be a small part of a well-diversified emergency fund. It's paramount that individuals assess their financial situation, risk tolerance, and the potential need for immediate access to their funds before considering this option. Regardless of the chosen vehicle for an emergency fund, the key is ensuring that the funds are accessible, secure, and separated from accounts used for everyday expenses.

Insurance Products: What You Really Need

Choosing the right insurance products is a crucial part of your financial safety net. It's vital to distinguish between essential insurance policies that offer you a layer of financial protection and those that might not be necessary for your current stage in life or financial situation. Health insurance, for example, is indispensable. It can shield you from the potentially catastrophic expenses of medical emergencies and treatments, illustrating its value as a fundamental necessity for everyone.

Another vital insurance coverage to consider is life insurance, especially if you have dependents. The primary purpose of life insurance is to provide financial security to your loved ones in the event of your untimely death, ensuring they are not burdened by debts or living costs. There are various forms of life insurance, with term life insurance offering a straightforward, cost-effective solution for many people. This type of insurance covers you for a specified period, paying out to your beneficiaries if you pass away within the term.

Homeowners or renters insurance also plays a critical role in your financial plan. For homeowners, this insurance not only covers your property in the event of damage from incidents like fires or natural disasters but also protects you against liability if someone is injured on your property. Renters aren't responsible for the building itself but still need to protect their personal property inside the rented space, which is where renters insurance comes in. Both types of policies help safeguard one of your most significant investments—your home and its contents.

Finally, disability insurance is an oft-overlooked aspect of financial planning that deserves attention. This type of insurance provides you with a portion of your income if you're unable to work due to a disability, whether temporary or permanent. Considering that your ability to earn an income is arguably your most valuable asset, insuring against the risk of losing that ability can be just as crucial as insuring physical possessions. Assessing your individual needs, lifestyle, and financial responsibilities will guide you in choosing the right mix of insurance products to protect you and your family's future.

Online Banking: Features and Benefits

Online banking, also known as internet banking, has revolutionized the way individuals manage their finances, offering unprecedented convenience and efficiency. This digital banking platform allows users to perform financial transactions via the internet, eliminating the need for physical visits to a bank branch. One of the most appealing aspects of online banking is its 24/7 accessibility, enabling customers to check their account balances, transfer funds, and pay bills anytime and from anywhere with an internet connection.

Security measures in online banking are a top priority, ensuring that users' financial information remains protected. Banks employ various security technologies, such as encryption, multi-factor authentication, and secure sockets layer (SSL) protocols, to safeguard sensitive data from unauthorized access. Although these measures significantly reduce the risk of cyber threats, users are also encouraged to practice safe online habits, such as regularly updating their passwords and avoiding unsecured Wi-Fi connections while conducting transactions.

Another significant benefit of online banking is its potential for better financial management through tools and features that many banks offer. These include budgeting tools, expense tracking, and alert systems for low balances or large transactions. Such capabilities not only provide users with a clearer picture of their financial health but also assist in making more informed decisions regarding spending and savings strategies. Furthermore, these tools can automate certain aspects of financial management, such as regular bill payments or savings transfers, further simplifying one's financial life.

Despite its numerous advantages, online banking is not without its critics. Some users may feel overwhelmed by the technology or prefer the personal interaction of traditional banking methods. However, many banks now offer comprehensive customer support for their online services, including live chat, email support, and detailed FAQs, to ease the transition for these customers. As technology continues to evolve, online banking is likely to become even more integrated into our daily lives, offering enhanced features and functionality to meet the growing demands of modern finance.

Cryptocurrency as an Investment

Cryptocurrency has stormed the financial market with its innovative approach to transactions and investments alike. As a digital or virtual currency that uses cryptography for security, it is decentralized and operates on a blockchain technology, a distributed ledger enforced by a disparate network of computers. This characteristic not only makes cryptocurrency difficult to counterfeit but also secures it from traditional governmental and financial institution controls, offering a new level of freedom and anonymity to users.

The allure of cryptocurrency as an investment lies primarily in its potential for significant returns. Bitcoin, for instance, the first and most well-known cryptocurrency, has experienced meteoric rises in value since its inception in 2009, capturing the attention of investors around the globe. Other cryptocurrencies, such as Ethereum, Ripple, and Litecoin, have similarly shown substantial growth over short periods. This volatility, while risky, provides the potential for high rewards, attracting traders and investors seeking to capitalize on price fluctuations.

However, the volatile nature of cryptocurrencies also presents a substantial risk. The market for cryptocurrencies is highly speculative, and prices can swing wildly in either direction due to factors like regulatory news, market sentiment, and the intrinsic unpredictability of a relatively new market. Such volatility can result in high losses as easily as it can yield significant gains, a fact that prospective investors must consider. Additionally, the regulatory environment for cryptocurrencies is still in development, with potential for significant changes that could impact their value and usability.

For those considering cryptocurrency as an investment, doing thorough research and employing a cautious approach is crucial. Understanding the technology behind cryptocurrencies, the security of the digital wallets used to store them, and the specific risks associated with their volatility and regulatory uncertainty are essential steps before investing. Diversification of one's investment portfolio to include a mix of traditional and digital assets can also mitigate potential losses. Despite the challenges, the innovation and potential that cryptocurrencies bring to the financial landscape continue to provide a compelling proposition for forward-thinking investors.

Peer-to-Peer (P2P) Lending: Revolutionizing Personal and Business Finance

Peer-to-peer (P2P) lending has emerged as a popular alternative to traditional banking and financial services, offering a platform for individuals and businesses to lend and borrow money directly from each other. By cutting out the middleman, P2P lending platforms provide borrowers with access to funds at competitive interest rates while offering lenders potentially higher returns on their investments. This article provides an overview of P2P lending, including how it works, its benefits, and some leading platforms where you can participate.

How Does P2P Lending Work?

P2P lending is facilitated by online platforms that connect borrowers seeking loans with investors willing to lend money. Borrowers apply for loans online, and their applications are evaluated using sophisticated algorithms that assess credit risk and determine an interest rate. Once approved, their loans are listed on the platform, allowing individual investors to fund either a portion or the entire amount of the loan. Borrowers then make monthly payments, which are distributed back to the investors as returns.

Benefits of P2P Lending

For Borrowers:

- **Lower Interest Rates**: Without the overhead costs of traditional banks, P2P platforms often offer lower interest rates.

- **Simplified Application Process**: The online application process is typically quick and user-friendly.

- **Access to Credit**: P2P lending can be a viable option for individuals who have difficulty securing loans from traditional banks.

For Investors:

- **Higher Returns**: Investors can often achieve higher returns on P2P platforms compared to traditional savings or investment products.

- **Diversification**: Investing in P2P loans can diversify an investment portfolio beyond traditional stocks and bonds.

- **Control**: Investors can choose which loans to fund, based on their own risk tolerance and investment criteria.

Leading P2P Lending Platforms

LendingClub

Website: https://www.lendingclub.com

One of the largest P2P lending platforms in the U.S., offering personal loans, business loans, and auto refinancing.

Prosper

Website: https://www.prosper.com

A pioneering P2P lending platform that offers personal loans for a variety of purposes, including debt consolidation and home improvements.

Funding Circle

Website: https://www.fundingcircle.com

Specializes in small business loans, offering fast approval and competitive rates for businesses looking to grow.

Peerform

Website: https://www.peerform.com

Focuses on personal loans with a wide range of interest rates, catering to borrowers with various credit scores.

What to Expect as a Participant

Borrowers: After completing an online application, you'll receive a loan offer that includes the interest rate and repayment terms. Once you accept, the loan will be funded by investors.

Investors: You'll need to create an account, deposit funds, and then you can start browsing available loans to invest in. Returns are received as borrowers repay their loans.

P2P lending offers a modern approach to borrowing and investing, characterized by its accessibility, efficiency, and potential for better rates for all parties involved. Whether you're looking to fund a personal project, grow your business, or invest your money in a new way, P2P lending platforms provide a valuable service. By carefully considering the terms and conducting due diligence, participants can make informed decisions and take full advantage of what P2P lending has to offer.

Financial Planning Services: When to Consider Professional Help

Deciding when to seek the assistance of financial planning services is a pivotal step in managing your financial future. These services are valuable not only for individuals with complex financial situations but also for those who want to ensure their financial planning is on the right track. Professional financial planners can offer advice on a wide range of topics, from investment management and retirement planning to tax strategies and estate planning. Their expertise can be instrumental in helping individuals and families achieve their long-term financial goals.

One common scenario where individuals may benefit from professional financial help is during significant life changes. These changes could include getting married, having a child, receiving a large inheritance, starting a business, or approaching retirement. During such times, the financial implications can be profound and multifaceted. A financial planner can provide valuable guidance that aligns with your long-term objectives, making these transitions smoother and financially sound.

Another factor to consider is your investment strategy. For those who are new to investing or have a substantial portfolio, navigating the complexities of the investment world can be daunting. Financial planners bring their market knowledge and can tailor an investment strategy that matches your risk tolerance and financial goals. They can also offer ongoing portfolio management, making adjustments as necessary to react to market changes or shifts in your financial situation.

Finally, as you approach retirement, the guidance of a financial planner becomes increasingly critical. Retirement planning involves a detailed evaluation of your current financial situation, expected retirement age, income sources, and lifestyle expectations. A financial planner can help you devise a comprehensive plan that maximizes your retirement savings, advises on Social Security benefits, and explores potential income streams. Their insight can make the difference between a comfortable retirement and financial stress during your golden years.

In conclusion, the decision to engage financial planning services should be based on your specific circumstances, future goals, and level of financial expertise. By offering tailored advice, financial planners can help you make informed decisions, avoid common pitfalls, and ultimately, achieve financial security and peace of mind. Whether you're navigating life changes, looking to optimize your investment strategy, or planning for retirement, professional guidance can be a valuable asset in your financial planning toolkit.

Chapter Seven

Investing in Financial Literacy and Support Networks

C hapter 7 of "The Hidden Money Manual" pivots towards an essential yet often overlooked aspect of financial health: investing in financial literacy and building robust support networks. It's a chapter designed not just for individual growth but to foster a community-oriented approach towards financial education. Herein lies the acknowledgment that wealth isn't merely a measure of money but a reflection of knowledge and communal support. This chapter dives deep into the concept that financial literacy should be seen as an ongoing investment in oneself, akin to investing in the stock market, real estate, or other assets. It argues that the dividends from this investment come in the form of better financial decisions, increased confidence in managing money, and ultimately, a more secure financial future.

Equally, the chapter shines a light on the significance of support networks - family, friends, mentors, and financial advisors - in navigating the complex world of finance. It posits that just as a tree relies on a network of roots to stand strong, individuals can significantly benefit from a foundation of support and shared knowledge. This support network can offer guidance during challenging times, share wisdom from their experiences, and provide a safety net when risks don't pan out as expected.

By integrating these two pillars, financial literacy and support networks, this chapter sets out to equip readers with the tools and community backing needed to not just survive but thrive in the financial aspects of their lives. It marks a shift from looking at financial management as a solitary task to viewing it as a shared journey, emphasizing that together, we can all reach greater heights of financial well-being.

Top Free Financial Literacy Websites: Empowering Your Financial Future

Financial literacy is crucial for making informed decisions about saving, investing, budgeting, and managing debt. Fortunately, numerous websites offer free resources to enhance your financial knowledge, regardless of your age or financial background. From interactive tools to comprehensive guides, these platforms provide valuable insights to help you navigate the complexities of personal finance. Here is a compilation of top free financial literacy websites that can empower you to take control of your financial future.

- **National Endowment for Financial Education (NEFE)**

- **Website**: https://www.nefe.org

- NEFE offers a wide range of resources designed to educate individuals at different life stages about financial planning, budgeting, and saving. Their High School Financial Planning Program is particularly noteworthy for young adults looking to get an early start on financial education.

- **Khan Academy**

  - **Website**: https://www.khanacademy.org

  - Khan Academy provides free, high-quality educational videos on a variety of subjects, including personal finance and economics. Their easy-to-understand videos cover topics from the basics of saving and investing to more complex concepts like cryptocurrency and estate planning.

- **MyMoney.gov**

  - **Website**: https://www.mymoney.gov

  - MyMoney.gov is a U.S. government website that consolidates financial education resources from over 20 federal websites in one place. It offers tools, articles, and checklists on managing money, understanding credit, and protecting against identity theft.

- **Investopedia**

  - **Website**: https://www.investopedia.com

○ Investopedia is a comprehensive resource for financial information and education. The website features thousands of articles, tutorials, and videos covering a wide array of financial topics, including investing, market news, strategies, and retirement planning.

- **Smart About Money**

  ○ **Website**: https://www.smartaboutmoney.org

  ○ Smart About Money, provided by the National Endowment for Financial Education, offers free courses, tools, and tips to help individuals make informed financial decisions. The website covers various aspects of personal finance, including emergencies, debt management, and work-life transitions.

- **The Simple Dollar**

  ○ **Website**: https://www.thesimpledollar.com

  ○ The Simple Dollar offers practical financial advice, tools, and resources to help readers manage their money more effectively. Topics range from frugal living and budgeting to investing and insurance, catering to a broad audience.

- **Financial Literacy and Education Commission (FLEC)**

  ○ **Website**: https://www.treasury.gov/resource-center/financial-education/Pages/commission-index.aspx

  ○ FLEC coordinates federal financial education efforts and

provides resources through its website. It's a valuable resource for finding government-backed financial education programs and initiatives.

- **Bogleheads**

  - **Website**: https://www.bogleheads.org

  - Inspired by the investment philosophy of Vanguard founder John Bogle, Bogleheads.org offers forums, articles, and a wiki where individuals can learn about low-cost investment strategies, retirement planning, and personal finance.

These free financial literacy websites offer a wealth of information and tools to help you understand and improve your financial situation. Whether you're a beginner looking to learn the basics or an experienced investor seeking advanced strategies, these resources can provide the knowledge you need to achieve your financial goals. By taking advantage of these free educational resources, you can empower yourself to make smarter financial decisions and build a stronger financial future.

Online Courses for Personal Finance: Elevating Your Financial Knowledge

In today's digital age, learning about personal finance has never been more accessible. With a plethora of online courses available, individuals can now deepen their understanding of financial management, investing, budgeting, and saving from the comfort of their own homes. These courses cater to a range of expertise levels, from beginners seeking to grasp the basics to advanced learners looking to refine their investment strategies. Below is a list of reputable platforms offering online courses in personal finance, designed to help you navigate your financial journey with confidence.

- Coursera

Website:

Coursera offers online courses from top universities and companies worldwide. Personal finance courses cover topics such as financial planning, investments, and behavioral finance. Courses are typically free to audit, with a fee to earn a certificate.

- Khan Academy

Website:

Renowned for its free learning resources, Khan Academy provides comprehensive courses on personal finance and economics, including savings and budgeting, homeownership, taxes, and retirement planning, all at no cost.

- Udemy

Website:

Udemy features a wide array of personal finance courses tailored to different needs, from basic financial literacy to specific investment techniques. While courses on Udemy are paid, they often run promotions offering significant discounts.

- edX

Website:

edX offers university-level courses in a wide range of disciplines, including personal finance, from prestigious institutions around the world. You can audit courses for free or pay a fee for a verified certificate.

- Alison

Website:

Alison provides free online courses on personal finance, covering subjects like financial literacy, budgeting, and planning for retirement. Courses are free to complete, with a fee for certificates.

- The Simple Dollar

Website: https://www.thesimpledollar.com/financial-wellness

While primarily a personal finance blog, The Simple Dollar offers a Financial Wellness course that covers fundamental personal finance topics, aiming to build a solid financial foundation for its readers.

- Investopedia Academy

Website: https://academy.investopedia.com

Investopedia Academy offers paid courses in various aspects of personal finance and investing. From beginner to advanced levels, these courses are designed to help individuals make informed financial decisions.

- Smart About Money

Website:

Provided by the National Endowment for Financial Education, Smart About Money offers free courses on a range of personal finance topics, designed to help you tackle financial challenges and build a healthier financial future.

Online courses in personal finance are an excellent way to enhance your financial literacy, offering the flexibility to learn at your own pace and on your own schedule. Whether you're aiming to get out of debt, invest wisely, or plan for retirement, there's a course out there to suit your needs. By taking advantage of these resources, you can gain the knowledge and confidence needed to make smart financial decisions and achieve your financial goals.

Personal Finance Podcasts and Blogs: Staying Informed on Your Financial Journey

In the ever-evolving world of personal finance, staying informed and motivated is key to achieving your financial goals. Personal finance podcasts and blogs offer a wealth of knowledge, from budgeting and saving tips to investment strategies and financial planning advice. Whether you're a beginner looking to build financial literacy or a seasoned investor seeking new insights, these resources can provide valuable guidance and inspiration. Below, we've compiled a list of notable personal finance podcasts and blogs that can help you navigate your financial journey.

Personal Finance Podcasts
The Dave Ramsey Show

- **Website**: https://www.ramseysolutions.com/shows/the-dave-ramsey-show

- Dave Ramsey offers practical advice for getting out of debt, saving money, and building wealth. His straightforward approach to managing money has helped millions achieve financial independence.

So Money with Farnoosh Torabi

- **Website**: http://podcast.farnoosh.tv

- Farnoosh Torabi hosts candid conversations with

world-renowned financial experts, authors, and influencers, offering insights on a wide range of financial topics, including personal finance, entrepreneurship, and lifestyle.

ChooseFI

- **Website**: https://www.choosefi.com

- Focused on the financial independence retire early (FIRE) movement, ChooseFI explores strategies for reducing expenses, paying off debt, and investing, aiming to help listeners achieve financial freedom.

The Money Guy Show

- **Website**: https://www.moneyguy.com

- Hosted by financial planners Brian Preston and Bo Hanson, The Money Guy Show dives into practical financial advice for all stages of life, emphasizing smart financial decision-making and wealth building.

Personal Finance Blogs
Mr. Money Mustache

- **Website**: https://www.mrmoneymustache.com

- Mr. Money Mustache is a blog about financial independence and early retirement. It offers advice on how to live a frugal yet fulfilling life, with tips on saving money, investing, and making smart financial choices.

The Financial Diet

- **Website**: https://thefinancialdiet.com

- The Financial Diet covers personal finance in a relatable and accessible way, targeting young adults. The blog discusses budgeting, career, lifestyle, and investing, aiming to make financial literacy more approachable.

Afford Anything

- **Website**: https://affordanything.com

- Paula Pant's Afford Anything focuses on building wealth and living life on your own terms. The blog challenges conventional wisdom on personal finance, real estate investing, and money management.

NerdWallet

- **Website**: https://www.nerdwallet.com/blog

- NerdWallet offers a broad range of financial advice, from credit cards and banking to investing and insurance. The blog provides in-depth reviews, comparisons, and personal finance tips to help readers make informed financial decisions.

Personal finance podcasts and blogs are invaluable resources for anyone looking to improve their financial well-being. By regularly engaging with these platforms, you can gain insights and strategies to manage your money more effectively, invest wisely, and achieve your financial goals. Whether through a podcast episode during your commute or a blog post over your morning coffee, these resources make financial education both accessible and engaging.

Joining Online Financial Communities: Enhancing Your Financial Journey

Online financial communities offer a platform for individuals to share experiences, seek advice, and gain insights into managing personal finances, investing, saving, and much more. These communities range from forums and social media groups to dedicated websites, catering to diverse interests and levels of expertise. By joining these communities, members can stay informed about the latest financial trends, tools, and strategies, benefiting from the collective wisdom of peers and experts alike. Here's an overview of how to engage with online financial communities, their benefits, and some popular platforms to consider.

Benefits of Joining Online Financial Communities

- **Knowledge Sharing**: Members share their successes and challenges, providing real-life insights into various financial strategies and products.

- **Support and Motivation**: Engaging with others who have similar financial goals can offer encouragement and motivation to stay on track with your financial plans.

- **Diverse Perspectives**: Interacting with a wide range of individuals can expose you to different viewpoints and strategies you may not have considered.

- **Resource Discovery**: Learn about tools, apps, books, and other resources that can aid in your financial journey.

How to Engage with Online Financial Communities

- **Participate Actively**: Join discussions, ask questions, and share your own experiences and insights.

- **Respect Community Rules**: Familiarize yourself with and adhere to the community's guidelines and etiquette.

- **Protect Your Privacy**: Be cautious about sharing personal or sensitive financial information.

- **Critically Evaluate Advice**: While communities can provide valuable advice, it's essential to research and consider the credibility of the information shared.

Popular Online Financial Communities to Consider

1. Reddit
- **Subreddits like r/personalfinance, r/investing, and r/financialindependence**

- Website: https://www.reddit.com

- Reddit hosts a variety of financial subreddits where users can ask questions, share advice, and discuss a wide range of topics from basic budgeting to advanced investing.

2. Bogleheads
- **Bogleheads Forum**

- Website: https://www.bogleheads.org/forum/

- Focused on the investing philosophy of John Bogle, founder of Vanguard, this community offers discussions on index fund investing, personal finance, and retirement planning.

3. Mr. Money Mustache Forum
- **MMM Community Forum**

- Website: https://forum.mrmoneymustache.com

- Centered around the financial independence and early retirement (FIRE) movement, this forum encourages frugal living and investing to achieve financial freedom.

4. Personal Finance Blogs and Forums
- **The Simple Dollar, Financial Samurai, and Early Retirement Extreme**

- These blogs often have active comments sections or associated forums where readers can engage in discussions, ask questions, and share experiences.

5. Facebook Groups
- **Search for personal finance, investing, and FIRE-related groups**

- Facebook hosts numerous groups dedicated to personal finance and investing, providing a platform for discussion, advice, and community support.

Joining an online financial community can be a transformative part of your financial journey. Whether you're seeking advice, motivation, or just a space to share your financial experiences, there's likely a community that fits your needs. By engaging with these communities, you can tap into a wealth of knowledge and support, helping you make informed decisions and progress towards your financial goals. Remember to approach advice with discernment and consider your own financial situation and objectives when participating.

Utilizing Library Resources for Financial Education: Uncovering Free Wealth-Building Tools

Public libraries stand as an invaluable yet often underutilized resource in the quest for financial literacy. They offer a wealth of materials and programs designed to aid in understanding and managing finances, all free of charge. From books and online databases to personal workshops and expert-led seminars, libraries equip you with the tools needed for making savvy financial decisions. Whether your focus is on effective budgeting, smart investing, or securing a comfortable retirement, tapping into your local library's offerings can significantly bolster your financial knowledge. Here's how to leverage these resources to your financial advantage, complete with website references for direct access.

Advantages of Library Resources for Financial Literacy

- **Comprehensive Learning Without the Price Tag**: Dive into an extensive array of financial education materials, including books, e-books, and online courses, all for free.

- **Tailored Guidance**: Benefit from workshops or personal consultations with financial advisors, courtesy of your library.

- **Varied Educational Content**: Access resources on a wide spectrum of financial topics, suitable for all levels of financial understanding, from novice to expert.

- **Engagement with Financial Communities**: Engage with financial seminars and workshops that bring together local financial professionals and community members.

Accessing Library Resources for Financial Education

- **Secure a Library Card**: Most public libraries offer free membership to local residents, unlocking access to a plethora of resources. Start by visiting your local library's website for membership details.

- **Browse the Online Catalog**: Utilize the library's online catalog to find resources on personal finance, including the latest books and digital publications.

  a. Example: https://www.worldcat.org for locating books in libraries near you.

- **Digital Databases and Learning Platforms**: Libraries often subscribe to financial databases and e-learning platforms, offering insights into investments, financial planning, and skill development.

  a. Example: https://www.lynda.com from LinkedIn, which may be available through your library's digital resources page.

- **Participate in Financial Education Programs**: Keep an eye on the library's events calendar for financial workshops, seminars, and other educational programs.

  a. Check your local library's events page for listings.

- **Consult with Librarians**: Don't overlook the wealth of knowledge librarians possess; they can direct you to the most useful resources based on your financial goals and queries.

Highlighted Financial Education Resources in Libraries
Books and E-Books

- Libraries boast a rich selection of personal finance books. For specific titles, explore https://www.goodreads.com for recommendations and then search your library's catalog.

Online Courses and Workshops

- Gain access to comprehensive online courses on financial topics through your library's affiliations with educational platforms. Additionally, many libraries organize in-person workshops with finance professionals.

Financial Magazines and Journals

- Keep abreast of the latest in finance by accessing periodicals like "Bloomberg Businessweek" or "Forbes" through library subscriptions.

Digital Learning Platforms

- Explore platforms such as Coursera (https://www.coursera.org) and Khan Academy (https://www.khanacademy.org) for courses on finance and economics, which might be available for free through your library's website.

Maximizing the resources available through public libraries can significantly enhance your financial literacy and empower you to make informed decisions. By exploring books, engaging in digital learning, and attending expert-led workshops, you gain access to a broad spectrum of financial knowledge and tools. Visit your local library online or in person to discover the vast resources at your disposal and take a proactive step toward mastering your financial future.

Mentorship in Personal Finance

Seeking mentorship is a potent pathway to deepen one's understanding of personal finance and accelerate financial growth. A mentor, drawing from their wealth of experience, can offer personalized guidance, strategic advice, and invaluable insight that textbooks or online courses may not provide. This relationship facilitates a hands-on approach to learning, allowing mentees to ask questions, avoid common pitfalls, and make smarter decisions. Mentorship in the realm of personal finance not only focuses on the mechanics of budgeting, investing, or saving but also imparts wisdom on navigating the psychological aspects of financial decision-making.

Finding a financial mentor can begin within one's personal network or through professional associations. Many experienced professionals are willing to share their knowledge and insights, recognizing the impact mentorship can have on an individual's financial health and overall life trajectory. Alternatively, virtual communities and online platforms offer access to mentorship opportunities, connecting individuals with mentors across the globe. It's important for mentees to seek out mentors whose financial goals and habits align with their own, ensuring a fruitful and compatible partnership.

The structure of a mentor-mentee relationship in personal finance can vary widely. Some may prefer regular, scheduled meetings, while others might benefit from a more flexible, as-needed communication style. Setting clear goals and expectations from the outset can help both parties maximize the efficiency and effectiveness of the relationship. A mentor can assist in setting realistic financial goals, developing a personalized plan to achieve them, and adjusting strategies as circumstances change.

Ultimately, the value of mentorship in personal finance cannot be overstated. It's about more than just acquiring knowledge; it's about gaining confidence, developing discipline, and cultivating a mindset geared towards financial independence and resilience. For those looking to enrich their financial literacy and competence, seeking out a mentor is a step in the right direction towards achieving personal and financial growth. By leveraging the insights and experiences of others, individuals can propel themselves towards their financial objectives with greater assurance and clarity.

Financial Wellness Workshops and Seminars

Beyond the one-on-one mentorship, financial wellness workshops and seminars stand as valuable resources for individuals aiming to bolster their financial literacy. These sessions, often led by financial experts and educators, cover a broad spectrum of topics ranging from basic budgeting skills to sophisticated investment strategies. By participating in these workshops, attendees can gain a comprehensive understanding of financial principles in a structured, community-driven environment. These events not only provide attendees with actionable knowledge but also foster a sense of camaraderie among participants who share similar financial goals. Furthermore, these seminars offer the unique advantage of direct interaction with financial professionals, allowing for the clarification of doubts and personalized advice. Engaging in such educational endeavors can significantly enhance one's financial competence, equipping individuals with the tools necessary to make informed and confident financial decisions.

YouTube Channels for Financial Advice: Navigating Your Finances Through Video Content

In the digital age, YouTube has become a vital source of information on a myriad of topics, including personal finance. With an abundance of channels dedicated to financial advice, viewers can find guidance on budgeting, investing, saving, and much more, all at their fingertips. These channels range from professional financial advisors to experienced individuals sharing their personal finance journeys. Here's a list of notable YouTube channels that offer valuable financial advice, complete with website URLs for easy access.

1. Graham Stephan

- **Channel**: <u>Graham Stephan</u>

- Graham Stephan discusses real estate investing, savings strategies, and wealth-building tips with a focus on financial independence. His approachable style makes complex financial concepts accessible to viewers of all levels.

2. The Financial Diet

- **Channel**: <u>The Financial Diet</u>

- The Financial Diet covers a wide range of topics, including budgeting, lifestyle changes for financial health, and tackling debt. Their content is particularly appealing to young adults looking to improve their financial literacy.

3. Dave Ramsey

- **Channel**: <u>Dave Ramsey</u>

- Dave Ramsey offers advice on debt freedom, emergency savings, and wealth building, following his well-known "7 Baby Steps" plan. His no-nonsense approach to personal finance has helped millions achieve financial peace.

4. Andrei Jikh

- **Channel**: <u>Andrei Jikh</u>

- Focusing on personal finance, investing, and the principles of financial minimalism, Andrei Jikh breaks down stock market investing and cryptocurrency in an engaging and understandable way.

5. Nate O'Brien

- **Channel**: Nate O'Brien

- Nate O'Brien shares insights on minimalist living, investing, and smart spending. His content is geared towards individuals looking to lead a frugal yet fulfilling lifestyle.

6. Investing with Rose

- **Channel**: Investing with Rose

- Rose focuses on investing strategies, stock market basics, and retirement planning. Her channel aims to demystify investing for beginners and encourages financial empowerment among women.

7. Michelle Schroeder-Gardner

- **Channel**: Michelle Schroeder-Gardner

- Known for her blog "Making Sense of Cents," Michelle shares advice on making and saving money, financial independence, and traveling full-time. Her practical tips are based on her own experiences of living a financially free life.

8. Minority Mindset

- **Channel**: Minority Mindset

- Jaspreet Singh discusses how to think differently about money, including strategies for increasing income, saving, and investing. The channel focuses on financial education and entrepreneurship.

YouTube's vast resource of financial advice channels offers something for everyone, from the novice saver to the seasoned investor. By subscribing to these channels, viewers can stay informed about the latest financial trends, learn new strategies for managing money, and be inspired by the personal finance journeys of others. Remember, while these channels provide valuable information, always conduct your own research and consider consulting with a financial professional before making significant financial decisions.

Financial Advice Apps: Streamlining Your Path to Financial Wellness

In the age of smartphones, financial advice apps have become indispensable tools for managing personal finances, offering a wealth of resources right at your fingertips. From budget tracking and investment advice to savings goals and debt management, these apps provide personalized financial guidance to help users make informed decisions. Whether you're looking to save more, invest wisely, or simply get a better handle on your spending, there's an app designed to meet your needs. Here's a rundown of some top financial advice apps available, complete with website URLs for more information.

1. Mint

- **Website**: https://www.mint.com

- Mint is one of the most popular budgeting apps, offering features for tracking spending, monitoring subscriptions, and setting financial goals. Its user-friendly interface makes managing your personal finances a breeze.

2. Personal Capital

- **Website**: https://www.personalcapital.com

- Personal Capital is geared more towards investors, providing tools for tracking investments, monitoring portfolio performance, and retirement planning. It's an excellent resource for a holistic view of your financial picture.

3. YNAB (You Need A Budget)

- **Website**: https://www.ynab.com

- YNAB stands out for its budgeting philosophy that emphasizes giving every dollar a job. It's designed to help users proactively manage their money, reduce debt, and live within their means.

4. Acorns

- **Website**: https://www.acorns.com

- Acorns simplifies investing by rounding up your daily purchases and investing the spare change. It's an ideal app for beginners looking to dip their toes into the world of investing without committing large sums of money.

5. Betterment

- **Website**: https://www.betterment.com

- Betterment is a robo-advisor app that offers automated investment advice based on your financial goals and risk tolerance. It's suitable for those who want to invest but prefer a hands-off approach.

6. Robinhood

- **Website**: https://www.robinhood.com

- Robinhood has revolutionized commission-free trading, allowing users to buy and sell stocks, ETFs, and cryptocurrencies without transaction fees. Its simple interface is attractive to novice and experienced traders alike.

7. PocketGuard

- **Website**: https://www.pocketguard.com

- PocketGuard helps users stay on top of their finances by tracking spending, identifying recurring subscriptions, and finding opportunities to save. Its goal is to help you optimize your spending and increase savings.

8. Wealthfront

- **Website**: https://www.wealthfront.com

- Wealthfront is another robo-advisor offering automated investment management and financial planning. Its features include tax-loss harvesting, portfolio rebalancing, and a cash account with a competitive interest rate.

Financial advice apps have transformed the way we manage our money, making it easier than ever to achieve financial wellness. By leveraging these tools, users can gain valuable insights into their financial habits, make smarter investment choices, and work towards their financial goals with confidence. Remember, while apps can provide powerful guidance and convenience, it's essential to choose one that aligns with your financial objectives and comfort level with technology.

Building a Personal Finance Book Collection

I've dedicated my career to uncovering and sharing the secrets of financial success and empowerment. My journey has not only been about exploring personal finance but also about discovering innovative ways for individuals to leverage their unique skills and resources for profit. Building a comprehensive book collection on personal finance is a fundamental step for anyone eager to navigate the complexities of money management, achieve financial independence, and explore new income opportunities. Here, I blend my insights with essential reads to guide you toward a well-rounded understanding of personal finance.

Essential Personal Finance Reads

"The Total Money Makeover" by Dave Ramsey offers a straightforward approach to debt elimination, emergency fund building, and wealth creation. It's foundational for anyone embarking on their financial freedom journey.

"Rich Dad Poor Dad" by Robert Kiyosaki has been instrumental in teaching the importance of investing in assets over liabilities, using the contrasting financial philosophies of my two dads as a framework.

"Your Money or Your Life" by Vicki Robin and Joe Dominguez goes beyond financial management, aligning spending with personal values to offer a comprehensive strategy for financial independence.

"I Will Teach You to Be Rich" by Ramit Sethi focuses on the pillars of personal finance: banking, saving, budgeting, and investing, making it indispensable for young adults navigating financial planning.

My Contributions to Your Personal Finance Library (Books by Gerry Marrs)

"How to Make Money Writing Product Reviews: Make Extra Money Getting Free Products Sent to Your Door" is my guide to monetizing your writing skills through product reviews. It's a step-by-step approach to creating engaging reviews, securing free products, and finding paying clients.

"Free Money For Nearly Anything: Start a Business, Buy a New Home, Free Benefits for Veterans" reveals how to access untapped funds and resources for various purposes without the need for loans.

"How to Legally Rob Credit-Card Companies: Get Out of Debt Faster, Raise Your Credit Score, and Finally Live Free!" provides strategies for navigating out of credit card debt, improving credit scores, and achieving financial freedom.

"How to Become a Profitable Money Broker: Make $100,000 per year assisting clients in finding low interest rate loans" guides you through building a lucrative career by connecting clients with low-interest loans for significant life events.

"How to Get Rich with Other People's Stuff: Make up to $5,000 per Month With Products You Don't Even Own!" explores establishing a home-based business and generating income through innovative methods like dropshipping and affiliate marketing, with minimal startup costs.

Building Your Collection

Curating a personal finance book collection that includes both foundational knowledge and innovative strategies is crucial for anyone looking to deepen their financial literacy and explore new avenues for income. My works, in particular, offer unique insights into leveraging modern opportunities for earning, complementing the timeless wisdom found in traditional personal finance literature. Together, these resources serve as a comprehensive toolkit for navigating your financial journey with confidence and creativity.

Chapter Eight

Building Towards Financial Security

I n Chapter 8, "Building Towards Financial Security," we pivot from immediate financial relief strategies and savings tactics to a more long-term perspective on financial health and stability. This chapter is dedicated to those who have started to see the fruits of their labor, having successfully employed the strategies outlined in previous chapters to find and save money. Here, we transition into the essential and often overlooked aspect of financial planning—building a resilient financial future. This chapter goes beyond mere saving; it is about strategically positioning yourself and your finances in such a way that you withstand and even thrive in the face of financial uncertainties. We will explore the importance of diversified investments, the basics of risk assessment, and the cultivation of a growth mindset towards personal finance. Expect to learn about creating robust financial plans that not only secure your present needs but also ensure your long-term prosperity. This chapter aims to guide you through the intricacies of financial security, empowering you to make informed decisions that lead you towards a secure financial future, untouched by the panic of potential economic downturns. Through the insights and practical advice provided here, you'll learn to build a financial safety net that can cushion you and your loved ones, ensuring peace of mind and the freedom to pursue your life's ambitions without monetary constraints.

Steps to Building an Emergency Fund

One of the foundational steps toward achieving financial security is the establishment of an emergency fund. This fund acts as a financial buffer that can save you in case of unexpected events such as job loss, medical emergencies, or urgent home repairs. The goal should be to save enough to cover three to six months of living expenses. This amount provides a cushion that allows you to maintain your lifestyle and commitments without the need to incur debt.

Building an emergency fund might seem daunting at first, especially if you're starting from scratch. However, by setting small, achievable goals, you can gradually build your fund over time. Begin by aiming to save $1,000, then incrementally increase your target as you reach each initial goal. Automatic transfers from your checking to your savings account can simplify the process, making saving effortless and ensuring consistency.

Another crucial aspect of building towards financial security involves understanding and managing debt. High-interest debt, particularly from credit cards, can be a significant barrier to financial stability. Prioritizing the repayment of these debts can free up resources that can then be directed towards your emergency fund or investments. Employ strategies like the debt snowball or avalanche methods to tackle your debts efficiently, focusing on paying off either the smallest balances first or those with the highest interest rates, respectively.

Finally, educating yourself on investment basics is fundamental to nurturing a resilient financial future. Investing is not reserved for the wealthy; it's a tool that can grow your wealth over time, even from modest beginnings. Diversifying your investments can reduce risk and increase potential returns, creating a more stable financial foundation. Consider low-cost index funds, bonds, and retirement accounts like 401(k)s or IRAs as starting points. Seeking advice from financial advisors or using robo-advisors can also demystify the process, helping you make informed decisions tailored to your financial goals and risk tolerance.

Automating Your Savings

Automating your savings is a powerful strategy to consistently grow your emergency fund without having to remember to make deposits manually. By setting up automatic transfers from your checking account to your savings account, you ensure that a designated amount of your income is saved each month. This method leverages the "out of sight, out of mind" principle, helping you to live within your means and potentially reducing the temptation to overspend. Many banks offer the option to set up automatic transfers, and you can choose a schedule that aligns with your payday to ensure you always have sufficient funds.

Furthermore, the approach of automating savings supports the concept of paying yourself first, a fundamental principle in personal finance. Before budgeting for expenses, entertainment, or discretionary purchases, you ensure that a portion of your income is dedicated to your future financial well-being. This habit not only accelerates the growth of your savings but also ingrains a strong financial discipline that can benefit you throughout your life.

The flexibility of automated savings is another significant advantage. You can start with a small amount and gradually increase it as your financial situation improves or as you become more comfortable with your budget. For instance, if you receive a raise, bonus, or tax refund, consider adjusting the amount transferred to savings to reflect your increased income. This incremental approach prevents the process from feeling overwhelming and allows you to adapt your savings plan as your financial goals evolve.

Lastly, integrating technology into your financial strategy through apps and online banking platforms can further enhance your savings efforts. Many financial institutions and fintech companies offer tools that round up your purchases to the nearest dollar and save the difference, or that analyze your spending habits and automatically save small amounts when you can afford it. Utilizing these tools in conjunction with automatic transfers can optimize your ability to save and invest, paving the way for a financially secure future.

Long-term Investment Strategies

Adopting a long-term perspective towards investing is essential for achieving financial security and realizing your future goals. A long-term investment strategy involves holding onto investments for several years, allowing your assets to grow and compound over time. This approach is particularly effective in riding out market volatility, as it focuses on the potential for growth over an extended period, rather than on short-term fluctuations. By committing to a long-term investment plan, investors are better positioned to build a substantial portfolio that can support their financial aspirations, whether for retirement, education funding, or other long-term objectives.

Diversification plays a pivotal role in long-term investment strategies. Spreading investments across a variety of asset classes, such as stocks, bonds, real estate, and commodities, can reduce risk and improve potential returns. Each asset class has its own set of risks and opportunities, and their performance can vary widely across different economic conditions. By diversifying, investors can mitigate the impact of poor performance in one area through gains in another, leading to more stable and consistent growth over time. Additionally, diversification can be personalized to match an investor's risk tolerance and investment horizon, making it a versatile tool in building a resilient investment portfolio.

The importance of patience and discipline cannot be overstated when it comes to long-term investing. Market downturns and economic uncertainties are inevitable, but they often present opportunities to buy quality assets at a lower price. However, succumbing to panic and selling off investments during these times can lock in losses and derail long-term financial plans. Maintaining a disciplined approach, adhering to your investment strategy, and keeping a long-term perspective during volatile periods can be challenging but is crucial for achieving investment success.

Finally, staying informed and periodically reviewing your investment strategy is important for long-term investment success. Financial markets and personal circumstances evolve, and an investment strategy that was once suitable may need adjustment. Regularly evaluating your portfolio, staying abreast of financial news and economic trends, and consulting with a financial professional can help ensure that your investment approach remains aligned with your goals. Adjustments may include rebalancing your portfolio to maintain your desired asset allocation or shifting your investment focus as you move closer to your financial goals. By staying proactive and adaptable, investors can enhance their ability to achieve long-term financial success.

The Basics of Estate Planning

Estate planning is a critical aspect of financial planning that involves arranging for the management and disposal of a person's estate during their lifetime and after death. Its importance cannot be overstated, as it ensures that your assets are distributed according to your wishes, potentially reduces estate taxes, and can prevent legal disputes among heirs. Essential components of estate planning include wills, trusts, a durable power of attorney, and healthcare directives. Each serves a specific purpose in safeguarding an individual's interests and those of their beneficiaries.

Creating a will is the first step in any comprehensive estate plan. A will is a legal document that outlines your wishes regarding the distribution of your assets and the care of any minor children. Without a will, the state laws determine these matters, which may not align with your intentions. Trusts, on the other hand, provide greater control over how and when your assets are distributed, allowing for more complex arrangements like providing for a disabled relative or ensuring financial support for minor children over time.

A durable power of attorney (POA) is another essential element of estate planning. It grants someone you trust the authority to make financial and legal decisions on your behalf should you become unable to do so due to illness or incapacity. This can include managing your investments, paying your bills, and overseeing your property. Similarly, a healthcare directive, sometimes known as a living will, outlines your wishes for medical treatment if you are unable to communicate your decisions. It can designate a healthcare proxy to make decisions on your behalf and specify your preferences regarding life-sustaining treatment.

Finally, it's important to note that estate planning is not a one-time task but an ongoing process. Life events such as marriage, the birth of a child, divorce, or the acquisition of significant assets necessitate revisiting and possibly updating your estate plan. Regularly reviewing and updating your estate documents ensures that your estate plan reflects your current wishes and circumstances, providing peace of mind for you and your loved ones. Engaging with a knowledgeable estate planning attorney can provide guidance tailored to your unique situation, ensuring that your estate plan effectively achieves your long-term goals and objectives.

Life and Disability Insurance Overview

Life and disability insurance play pivotal roles in comprehensive estate planning, serving as crucial safeguards for your financial security and that of your loved ones. Life insurance, in particular, offers monetary support to your beneficiaries after your passing, helping manage debts, cover funeral expenses, and provide for your family's future needs. The type of life insurance policy—whether term, whole, or universal—can be selected based on your specific financial goals and the needs of your dependents. It's vital to assess the amount of coverage necessary to ensure your family's lifestyle and future expenses are adequately supported without your economic contribution.

Disability insurance, on the other hand, offers income protection should you become unable to work due to injury or illness. This type of insurance is crucial for maintaining your lifestyle and meeting your financial obligations in the event of unforeseen medical circumstances that prevent you from earning an income. Short-term and long-term disability policies cater to different needs, with the former providing immediate financial assistance for a limited period, usually up to a year, and the latter offering extended coverage that can last from several years to the rest of your life.

Choosing the right insurance policies requires a careful analysis of your current financial situation, future goals, and potential risks. Factors to consider include your current income, the standard of living you wish to maintain for your family, existing debts, and your overall estate planning objectives. Insurance is not merely a financial product but a fundamental component of a holistic estate plan designed to protect and provide for your family's future.

Finally, regular review and adjustments to your life and disability insurance coverage are as necessary as they are for your broader estate plan. Changes in income, marital status, the birth of children, and other significant life events may impact your insurance needs. Working with a financial advisor or insurance professional can help you assess and update your policies, ensuring they align with your evolving estate planning goals. This proactive approach guarantees that you and your loved ones are adequately protected, no matter what the future holds.

Retirement Planning Tools and Resources: Navigating Your Way to a Secure Future

Retirement planning is a crucial aspect of financial management, requiring careful consideration and strategic planning. With the right tools and resources, preparing for retirement can be a less daunting task, allowing individuals to map out a secure financial future with confidence. This article explores a selection of the best retirement planning tools and resources available today, each designed to assist you in different aspects of your retirement planning journey.

Online Calculators and Software

1. Vanguard Retirement Income Calculator Website: Vanguard offers a comprehensive retirement income calculator that helps users estimate how much income they could expect from their retirement savings. By inputting details about your savings, investment style, and retirement goals, you can get a personalized estimate of your retirement income.

2. Personal Capital Retirement Planner Website: Personal Capital's Retirement Planner allows users to link their accounts for a real-time view of their financial status. This tool uses your actual financial data to run various retirement scenarios and assess the impact of different financial decisions on your retirement readiness.

Investment Platforms

3. Betterment Website: Betterment is an online investment platform that offers retirement planning services among its suite of tools. It provides personalized investment advice based on your retirement goals and risk tolerance, simplifying the process of building a retirement-focused investment portfolio.

4. Fidelity Investments Website: Fidelity offers a wide range of resources for retirement planning, including investment advice, retirement accounts, and an array of online tools and calculators. Their services cater to both individuals planning for retirement and those already in retirement, seeking to manage their income and investments.

Educational Resources

5. Investopedia Retirement Planning Website: https://www.investopedia.com/retirement/Investopedia provides a comprehensive guide to retirement planning, covering topics from the basics of retirement savings to advanced investment strategies. It's an excellent resource for both beginners and experienced investors looking to deepen their understanding of retirement planning.

6. AARP Retirement Planning Website: https://www.aarp.o rg/retirement/AARP offers a wealth of information on retirement planning, social security, and Medicare. Their resources are particularly valuable for those approaching retirement age, providing guidance on everything from health insurance to retirement income strategies.

Government Resources

7. Social Security Administration Website: The SSA website provides tools and calculators to estimate your social security benefits at various retirement ages. It's an essential resource for understanding how social security benefits fit into your overall retirement plan.

8. Internal Revenue Service (IRS) Retirement Plans Website: https://www.irs.gov/retirement-plansThe IRS offers guidance on retirement plan options, tax implications, and contribution limits. It's a critical resource for navigating the tax aspects of retirement savings and investments.

Planning for retirement doesn't have to be an overwhelming process. With the right tools and resources, you can gain clarity on your retirement goals and create a plan to achieve them. Whether you're starting to save for retirement, looking to invest wisely, or nearing retirement and planning for income, these tools and resources provide valuable support at every stage of your retirement planning journey. By taking advantage of these platforms, calculators, and educational materials, you're taking an important step toward securing a financially stable and fulfilling retirement.

Debt-Free Living Strategies

Debt-free living is a financial goal for many individuals, encompassing a lifestyle that avoids the reliance on borrowing and focuses on building a solid financial foundation. Achieving a debt-free status is not only liberating but also promotes a sense of financial security and independence. The first step towards this goal involves creating a comprehensive budget. This financial plan enables you to track your income and expenses, ensuring that you live within your means. By prioritizing essential expenses and reducing unnecessary spending, you can allocate more resources toward paying off existing debts.

Building an emergency fund is another crucial component of debt-free living. This fund acts as a financial safety net, preventing the need to borrow money in case of unexpected expenses such as medical bills or car repairs. Financial experts recommend saving at least three to six months' worth of living expenses. This fund contributes to financial stability by providing a buffer against life's unpredictable moments, allowing you to maintain your debt-free lifestyle without compromising your financial health.

Reducing debt also involves adopting strategies to pay off existing obligations more efficiently. The snowball and avalanche methods are popular approaches. The snowball method involves paying off debts from smallest to largest, regardless of interest rate, to build momentum and motivation. Conversely, the avalanche method prioritizes debts with the highest interest rates, minimizing the amount paid in interest over time. Both strategies require discipline and a commitment to consistent payments, but they can significantly accelerate the path to living debt-free.

Once debt is under control or eliminated, the focus shifts to wealth building. Investing in retirement accounts, such as a 401(k) or an individual retirement account (IRA), can secure your financial future. Real estate, stocks, and bonds are other avenues to consider.

The goal should be to create a diversified investment portfolio that matches your risk tolerance and financial objectives. Living debt-free isn't merely about avoiding loans and credit cards; it's about establishing a financial strategy that supports your long-term well-being. By following these guidelines and leveraging financial planning tools and resources, you can chart a course towards a debt-free and financially secure future.

Homeownership vs. Renting Decisions

Choosing between homeownership and renting is a pivotal financial decision. Homeownership is often seen as a hallmark of financial stability and independence, offering the potential for property value appreciation and the ability to personalize one's living space. Additionally, owning a home can serve as a forced savings plan, with each mortgage payment increasing equity. This financial stake in a property can prove lucrative over the long term, especially in a robust real estate market. However, homeowners also bear the full responsibility for maintenance costs, property taxes, and insurance, which can add significant expenses beyond the monthly mortgage payment.

On the other hand, renting offers flexibility and mobility that homeownership cannot match. For individuals and families who prioritize location over space or who may need to move frequently for work, renting can be a more practical choice. It also relieves tenants of the financial burdens associated with repairs and maintenance, as these responsibilities fall to the landlord. Renting can also be a strategic financial choice for those saving towards buying a home in the future or investing in other financial ventures that may offer quicker or higher returns than real estate.

The decision between renting and buying also significantly hinges on current market conditions and long-term financial goals. In markets where housing prices are high and inventory is low, the barrier to entry for first-time homebuyers can be daunting. High interest rates can further complicate affordability, making renting a more viable option for many. Conversely, in a buyer's market, where housing prices are more accessible, and mortgage rates are favorable, buying a home could be a wise investment.

Ultimately, the choice between homeownership and renting is deeply personal and should align with one's lifestyle, financial situation, and future goals. It requires careful consideration of the costs, benefits, and responsibilities associated with each option. Consulting with a financial advisor to review one's financial health and housing needs can provide valuable insight into making this significant decision.

College Savings Plans for Children

Preparing for a child's future, especially in terms of education, is a monumental task that requires careful planning and consideration. One of the most effective ways parents can secure their child's academic future is by investing in a college savings plan. These plans come in various forms, most notably the 529 plans and Coverdell Education Savings Accounts (ESAs), each offering distinct benefits and limitations. Understanding the nuances of these savings vehicles can empower parents to make informed decisions that align with their financial capabilities and educational aspirations for their children.

The 529 Plan is widely regarded for its tax advantages and flexible contribution limits. Earnings in a 529 plan grow tax-free, and withdrawals for qualified education expenses are not taxed. This feature makes it an attractive option for parents looking to maximize their investment in their child's education. Furthermore, 529 plans are not limited to tuition but can also be used for room and board, books, and other educational expenses. Some states even offer tax deductions or credits for contributions, enhancing the appeal of this savings option.

On the other hand, Coverdell ESAs offer a more restricted contribution limit but provide broader flexibility in how the funds can be used. With a maximum contribution of $2,000 per year, ESAs are not as robust as 529 plans in terms of investment growth potential. However, they do allow for expenses associated with K-12 education in addition to college expenses, which includes tuition, uniforms, and even computers. This makes ESAs particularly appealing for parents who envision private schooling or anticipate early educational expenses for their children.

Deciding between a 529 plan and an ESA, or perhaps utilizing a combination of both, requires a strategic approach to planning for a child's educational future. Factors such as state residency, financial situation, and the intended use of funds play critical roles in this decision-making process. It's also crucial for parents to regularly review and adjust their savings strategy as their financial situation evolves and as their child gets closer to college age. Consulting with a financial advisor can provide tailored advice and insights, helping families to effectively prepare for the significant investment of a college education.

Creating a Financial Legacy

Investing in a child's education goes beyond the present; it's about building a foundation that supports their future success and well-being. The process of saving for education is not just about accumulating a sum of money but also about creating a financial legacy. This legacy is a reflection of values, aspirations, and the importance of education in family culture. Parents and guardians have the opportunity to teach their children about financial responsibility, the value of education, and planning for the future through their savings efforts.

Choosing the right savings plan is akin to selecting the best tools for crafting this legacy. While 529 plans offer significant growth potential and tax advantages, making them an attractive option for many families, Coverdell ESAs provide the flexibility needed for those who prioritize educational diversity and early educational investments. Each plan has its merits and limitations, indicating that the choice highly depends on individual family needs, preferences, and financial situations.

In addition to selecting the appropriate savings vehicle, it's paramount for families to consider the long-term implications of their savings strategy. This includes understanding how their chosen plan impacts financial aid eligibility, the tax implications of withdrawals for educational expenses, and how the account will be managed should it exceed the needs of the beneficiary. An often overlooked but critical aspect of creating a financial legacy is ensuring that there's a plan in place for any unused funds, whether it's changing the beneficiary within the family or understanding any tax liabilities or penalties involved in non-educational withdrawals.

To this end, engaging with a financial advisor can be a crucial step in navigating the complex landscape of educational savings. A professional can offer insights tailored to the unique circumstances of each family, highlight opportunities for maximizing savings, and help avoid common pitfalls. By taking a proactive and informed approach to saving for education, families can ensure that their financial legacy is both impactful and enduring, paving the way for future generations' educational and financial success.

Appendix A: Financial Planning Templates

Budget Worksheet

The Budget Worksheet, included in Appendix A, is designed as a user-friendly tool to help readers meticulously organize their income and expenses. This interactive template not only guides individuals through the process of tracking their monthly financial activities but also highlights areas where they can potentially cut costs or find opportunities for additional income. By regularly updating and reviewing their Budget Worksheet, users can maintain a clear overview of their financial health, make informed decisions, and set realistic goals towards achieving financial stability and growth.

#	Source	Amount	Type	Category	Description
1	Salary	3000			
2	Freelance Work	500			
3	Investment Returns	200			
4	Other	100			
5		-1200	Rent/Mortgage		
6		-300	Utilities		
7		-400	Groceries		
8		-150	Transportation		
9		-200	Insurance		
10		-100	Entertainment		
11		-250	Miscellaneous		
12		3800		Income	Total Monthly Income
13		-2600		Expenses	Total Monthly Expenses
14		1200		Net Savings	Income - Expenses

Budget Worksheet

This worksheet includes:

- **Income Sources:** Salary, Freelance Work, Investment Returns, Other.

- **Expenses:** Categorized into Rent/Mortgage, Utilities, Groceries, Transportation, Insurance, Entertainment, Miscellaneous.

- **Summary:** Total Monthly Income, Total Monthly Expenses, and Net Savings calculated from the total income and expenses.

Each category (Income, Expenses) is totaled to reflect in the Summary section, showing a clear picture of financial health for the month. This example can be tailored to match your specific financial situation by adjusting the categories and amounts as necessary.

Expense Tracker

An Expense Tracker is a detailed log designed to record every transaction you make, capturing the essence of where your money goes daily. By meticulously tracking each expense, you can gain insights into your spending habits, identify areas where you can cut back, and make informed decisions about your finances. This tool is crucial for anyone looking to manage their money more effectively, save for goals, or simply understand their financial habits better.

Key Features of an Expense Tracker:

- **Date of Transaction:** Allows you to see when you spent the money.

- **Amount:** The cost of each transaction, showing how much you spent.

- **Category:** Helps in classifying expenses (e.g., groceries, utilities, dining out) for better analysis of spending patterns.

- **Payment Method:** Tracks whether the payment was made with cash, credit, debit, or any other form of payment.

- **Description/Notes:** Provides space to add details about each expense, offering context and reminders for future reference.

Benefits:

- **Budget Management:** Helps in sticking to a budget by providing real-time insight into where your money is going.

- **Spending Insights:** Reveals patterns in your spending habits, potentially highlighting areas where you can save.

- **Goal Tracking:** Supports financial goals by making you more mindful of unnecessary expenses.

- **Expense Categorization:** Assists in understanding how much is spent on different areas of life, such as food, entertainment, or bills.

- Here's an example of an **Expense Tracker** presented as a spreadsheet:

Date	Amount	Category	Payment Method	Description/Notes
2024-02-01	-45.50	Groceries	Debit Card	Weekly groceries
2024-02-02	-19.95	Utilities	Credit Card	Monthly electric bill
2024-02-03	-13.99	Entertainment	Cash	Movie rental
2024-02-04	-29.99	Transportation	Credit Card	Gas for car
2024-02-05	-3.50	Snacks	Cash	Coffee

Expense Tracker

Debt Repayment Plan

A Debt Repayment Plan is a strategic approach to paying off outstanding debts in an efficient and organized manner. It involves listing all of your debts, including information such as the creditor's name, the total amount owed, the interest rate, and the minimum monthly payment required. The plan outlines a method for repayment that prioritizes debts, often focusing on either the highest interest rates first (the debt avalanche method) or the smallest debts first (the debt snowball method), to reduce the total interest paid or to quickly reduce the number of creditors, respectively.

Key Components of a Debt Repayment Plan:

- **Creditor Name:** Who you owe the money to.

- **Total Amount Owed:** The full amount you need to repay.

- **Interest Rate:** The rate at which the debt will accrue interest.

- **Minimum Monthly Payment:** The least amount you can pay each month without penalties.

- **Proposed Payment:** Your planned monthly payment that may be higher than the minimum to expedite repayment.

- **Due Date:** When the payment is due each month.

Benefits of a Debt Repayment Plan:
- **Clear Repayment Strategy:** Provides a structured approach to becoming debt-free.

- **Interest Savings:** Can significantly reduce the amount of interest paid over time.

- **Motivation:** Offers psychological wins by clearing individual debts.

- **Financial Health:** Improves your credit score and financial stability by systematically reducing debt.

Let's create a spreadsheet-based example of a Debt Repayment Plan. This example will include a list of debts with the details mentioned above, offering a visual representation of how to organize and prioritize debt repayment.

Here's an example of a **Debt Repayment Plan** presented as a spreadsheet:

Creditor Name	Total Amount Owed	Interest Rate (%)	Minimum Monthly Payment	Proposed Payment	Due Date
Credit Card Co	5000	19.99	150	200	2024-03-05
Student Loan	20000	5.5	220	220	2024-03-15
Auto Loan	15000	3.75	280	280	2024-03-22
Personal Loan	4000	7.5	85	100	2024-03-30

Debt Repayment Plan

This table outlines a strategic approach to debt repayment, including essential details like the creditor's name, total amount owed, interest rate, minimum monthly payment, and a proposed payment that's higher than the minimum for the highest interest debt. This plan also includes the due dates for each payment, helping to manage cash flow and ensure payments are made on time.

By focusing on the debt with the highest interest rate first (in this case, the Credit Card Co), extra payments are allocated to reduce the principal balance faster, thereby saving on interest costs over time. This methodical approach provides a clear path toward financial freedom, improving your credit score and reducing financial stress as debts are paid off.

Savings Goal Tracker

A Savings Goal Tracker is a useful tool for managing and monitoring progress towards a financial target, such as building an emergency fund, saving for a vacation, or accumulating a down payment for a home. It helps you set clear savings goals, track your contributions, and stay motivated by visualizing your progress. Utilizing a spreadsheet for this purpose can make the process more organized, accessible, and efficient.

How to Create a Savings Goal Tracker in a Spreadsheet

Step 1: Define Your Savings Goal

Start by clearly defining your savings goal. Include the total amount you need and the deadline by which you want to achieve this goal. This information will be the foundation of your tracker.

Step 2: Setup Your Spreadsheet

Open your preferred spreadsheet software (like Microsoft Excel or Google Sheets) and create a new document. Set up the following columns to organize your tracker:

1. **Date**: The date of each contribution or withdrawal.

2. **Description**: A brief note about the transaction.

3. **Amount**: The amount saved or withdrawn.

4. **Running Total**: A cumulative total of your savings.

5. **Goal Amount**: Your total savings goal (this will be a static number across all rows).

6. **Remaining**: The difference between your goal amount and the running total.

Step 3: Input Your Data

Start entering your savings data as you make contributions. Each row will represent a different transaction. Use the spreadsheet's formulas to calculate the Running Total and Remaining amounts automatically.

- **Running Total Formula**: For the first row, this will simply be the amount in the same row. For subsequent rows, it will be the sum of the previous row's Running Total and the current row's Amount.

- **Remaining Formula**: Subtract the Running Total from the Goal Amount.

Step 4: Visualize Your Progress

Many spreadsheet applications allow you to create charts. Use this feature to create a visual representation of your progress towards your goal. A line graph plotting the Running Total against time or a bar chart comparing your progress to the goal can be very motivational.

Example Spreadsheet Layout

Here is a simple layout for a Savings Goal Tracker:

Date	Description	Amount	Running Total	Goal Amount	Remaining
2024-01-01	Initial Deposit	$500	$500	$5,000	$4,500
2024-01-15	Bi-weekly Savings	$250	$750	$5,000	$4,250
...	...	...	...	...	...

Savings Goal Tracker

Spreadsheet Formulas

- **Running Total**: In cell D2, input =**C2**. In cell D3, input =**D2+C3** and drag the formula down for each new entry.

- **Remaining**: In cell F2 (and the entire column), input =**E2-D2** to calculate the remaining amount needed to reach your goal, and drag this formula down.

A Savings Goal Tracker spreadsheet is an excellent method to stay on top of your financial objectives. It not only provides clarity and organization but also offers a visual reminder of your progress, which can greatly enhance your motivation to save. With regular updates and reviews, you can adjust your savings plan as needed to ensure you meet your goals.

Financial Goal Setting Worksheet

A Financial Goal Setting Worksheet is an instrumental tool in planning and achieving financial objectives. It helps individuals or families articulate their financial aspirations, prioritize them, and develop actionable steps towards realizing these goals. Unlike a Savings Goal Tracker that focuses on tracking progress towards a specific financial target, a Financial Goal Setting Worksheet encompasses a broader scope, including identifying various goals, setting timeframes, estimating costs, and planning for income and expenses.

How to Create a Financial Goal Setting Worksheet in a Spreadsheet

Step 1: Identify Your Financial Goals

Begin by listing all your financial goals, both short-term (within a year), medium-term (1-5 years), and long-term (5+ years). These could range from saving for a vacation, paying off debt, to retirement savings.

Step 2: Setup Your Spreadsheet

Open your preferred spreadsheet application and create a new document. Organize your worksheet with the following columns to capture the details of each financial goal:

1. **Goal**: The name of the financial goal.

2. **Priority**: Importance of the goal (High, Medium, Low).

3. **Cost Estimate**: An estimate of how much money is needed to achieve the goal.

4. **Timeframe**: The target date or duration to achieve the goal.

5. **Monthly Savings Target**: The amount needed to save each month to meet the goal within the specified timeframe.

6. **Current Savings**: How much you have already saved towards this goal.

7. **Remaining**: The difference between the Cost Estimate and Current Savings.

Step 3: Fill in Your Goals

List each of your financial goals in the spreadsheet, along with their priority, cost estimate, and timeframe. This overview will help you see the big picture and start planning effectively.

Step 4: Calculate Monthly Savings Targets and Remaining Amounts

Use spreadsheet formulas to calculate how much you need to save each month for each goal and what remains to be saved.

- **Monthly Savings Target Formula**: Divide the Cost Estimate by the number of months in the Timeframe.

- **Remaining Formula**: Subtract Current Savings from the Cost Estimate.

Step 5: Plan for Action

With all the information laid out, you can start to plan how to allocate your income towards these goals, considering your priorities and what is realistically achievable within your budget.

Example Spreadsheet Layout

Here's a simple template layout for a Financial Goal Setting Worksheet:

Goal	Priority	Cost Estimate	Timeframe	Monthly Savings Target	Current Savings	Remaining
Emergency Fund	High	$10,000	12 months	$833.33	$2,000	$8,000
Vacation	Medium	$3,000	6 months	$500	$500	$2,500
Pay off Credit Card	High	$5,000	12 months	$416.67	$1,000	$4,000
Retirement Savings	Low	-	-	Variable	-	-

Financial Goal Setting Worksheet

Spreadsheet Formulas

- **Monthly Savings Target**: In cell E2, input =**C2/D2*12** (if Timeframe is in years) or =**C2/D2** (if Timeframe is in months), adjusting for each goal's specifics.

- **Remaining**: In cell G2, input =**C2-F2** for calculating the remaining amount to save.

A Financial Goal Setting Worksheet in a spreadsheet format offers a structured and clear method to map out your financial future. By breaking down your goals into actionable steps and understanding the financial commitment required for each, you can prioritize effectively and make informed decisions on how to allocate your resources. Regularly reviewing and updating your worksheet can also help you stay on track and adjust your plans as your financial situation changes.

Monthly Financial Overview

A Monthly Financial Overview is a comprehensive snapshot of your finances for a given month, providing insight into your income, expenses, savings, and financial health. This tool is crucial for budgeting effectively, identifying potential areas for savings, and making informed decisions about your financial future. A well-organized

Monthly Financial Overview allows you to see where your money is going, how much you're saving, and where you might need to adjust your spending habits.

How to Create a Monthly Financial Overview in a Spreadsheet

Step 1: Gather Financial Data

Collect all relevant financial information for the month, including all sources of income, fixed expenses (rent, mortgage, insurance), variable expenses (groceries, entertainment), savings, and any debts or loans.

Step 2: Setup Your Spreadsheet

Open your preferred spreadsheet software and create a new document. Organize your spreadsheet with the following sections:

1. **Income**: List all sources of income and the total income for the month.

2. **Fixed Expenses**: List all fixed expenses and the total fixed expenses.

3. **Variable Expenses**: List all variable expenses and the total variable expenses.

4. **Savings**: Detail any contributions to savings accounts or investments.

5. **Summary**: Provide a summary section that includes Total Income, Total Expenses (Fixed + Variable), Net Savings (Income - Total Expenses), and Remaining Balance.

Step 3: Input Your Data

Fill in each section with your financial data for the month. Be as detailed as possible to ensure accuracy.

Step 4: Calculate Totals and Summaries

Use spreadsheet formulas to calculate the totals for each section and the summary metrics. This will give you a clear picture of your financial activity for the month.

Step 5: Analyze and Plan

With your Monthly Financial Overview complete, analyze the data to identify trends, potential areas for savings, and opportunities for financial improvement. Use this analysis to plan for future months, adjusting your budget and savings goals as necessary.

Example Spreadsheet Layout

Here is a simplified layout for a Monthly Financial Overview:

Section	Description	Amount
Income		
Salary	Main job	$3,000
Freelance	Freelance work	$500
Total Income		**$3,500**
Fixed Expenses		
Rent	Apartment rent	$1,000
Insurance	Health insurance	$200
Total Fixed Expenses		**$1,200**
Variable Expenses		
Groceries	Food and supplies	$300
Entertainment	Movies, dining out	$150
Total Variable Expenses		**$450**
Savings		
Savings Account	Monthly savings	$500
Summary		
Total Income		$3,500
Total Expenses		$1,650
Net Savings		$1,850
Remaining Balance		$1,850

Monthly Financial Overview

Spreadsheet Formulas

- **Total Income/Expenses**: Use the **SUM** function to calculate the total income, fixed expenses, and variable expenses.

For example, **=SUM(B2:B3)** for Total Income.

- **Net Savings**: Subtract Total Expenses from Total Income. For example, **=B10-B14** (assuming Total Income is in B10 and Total Expenses in B14).

- **Remaining Balance**: This might equal Net Savings if all excess income is saved, or it may need to be adjusted based on additional financial activities not captured elsewhere.

Creating a Monthly Financial Overview in a spreadsheet is a powerful way to keep track of your financial situation, allowing for better financial planning and decision-making. By regularly updating and reviewing this overview, you can stay on top of your finances, adjust your budget as necessary, and work towards your financial goals with clarity and confidence.

Credit Score Monitoring Chart

A Credit Score Monitoring Chart is an effective tool for tracking your credit score over time, helping you understand how your financial behaviors impact your creditworthiness. Regularly monitoring your credit score is essential for maintaining good financial health, as it affects your ability to borrow money, secure favorable interest rates, and sometimes even get a job or rent an apartment. A spreadsheet can serve as a simple yet powerful means to visually track changes in your credit score, identify trends, and set goals for improvement.

How to Create a Credit Score Monitoring Chart in a Spreadsheet

Step 1: Collect Your Credit Score Data

Start by gathering your credit score data. You can obtain your credit score from various sources, including credit bureaus, banks, or credit monitoring services. It's helpful to collect this data periodically (e.g., monthly or quarterly).

Step 2: Setup Your Spreadsheet

Open your preferred spreadsheet software (like Microsoft Excel or Google Sheets) and create a new document. Organize your spreadsheet with the following columns:

1. **Date**: The date when the credit score was recorded.

2. **Credit Score**: Your credit score on that date.

3. **Source**: The source from where the credit score was obtained (optional).

4. **Notes**: Any relevant notes or factors that might have influenced your credit score, such as opening a new credit line, paying off a loan, or any discrepancies you noticed.

Step 3: Input Your Data

Fill in the data you've collected for each period you have a credit score available. Be consistent with the time intervals for a meaningful trend analysis.

Step 4: Create a Chart

Highlight your data and insert a line chart to visualize your credit score over time. This graphical representation will make it easier to spot trends, fluctuations, and the overall direction of your credit health.

Step 5: Analyze and Plan

Use the chart to identify patterns or events that positively or negatively affect your credit score. This insight can help you make informed decisions to improve or maintain your credit score, such as reducing credit card balances, paying bills on time, or avoiding hard inquiries.

Example Spreadsheet Layout

Here is a simplified layout for a Credit Score Monitoring Chart:

Date	Credit Score	Source	Notes
2024-01-01	720	Credit Bureau	Paid off car loan
2024-02-01	730	Bank	Reduced credit card debt
2024-03-01	725	Credit Bureau	Hard inquiry for mortgage
...	...	...	...

Credit Score Monitoring Chart

Visual Representation

After populating the spreadsheet with your data, you can create a line chart to visually track your credit score progression over time. This chart will plot the "Date" on the X-axis and "Credit Score" on the Y-axis, providing a clear visual trend of your credit score movements.

A Credit Score Monitoring Chart in a spreadsheet is a straightforward and effective way to keep an eye on your credit score changes over time. By systematically tracking and analyzing your credit score, you can take proactive steps to improve your financial health, plan for the future, and ensure you're in the best position to take advantage of financial opportunities as they arise.

Investment Portfolio Tracker

An Investment Portfolio Tracker is a dynamic tool designed to monitor and manage your investment portfolio over time. It helps investors keep track of various assets, including stocks, bonds, mutual funds, ETFs, and other investments, to understand their portfolio's performance, asset allocation, and risk exposure. By using a spreadsheet for this purpose, investors can customize their tracker to suit their specific needs, enabling them to make informed decisions based on comprehensive data analysis.

How to Create an Investment Portfolio Tracker in a Spreadsheet

Step 1: Define Your Portfolio Components

List all the investments you hold, categorizing them by type (e.g., stocks, bonds, mutual funds). This categorization will help in analyzing the diversification and risk of your portfolio.

Step 2: Setup Your Spreadsheet

Open your preferred spreadsheet software and set up your document with the following columns to capture key data about each investment:

1. **Investment Name**: The name or ticker symbol of the investment.

2. **Category**: The type of investment (stocks, bonds, etc.).

3. **Purchase Date**: When you acquired the investment.

4. **Quantity**: The number of shares or units you own.

5. **Purchase Price**: The price at which you bought each share or unit.

6. **Current Price**: The current market price of each share or unit.

7. **Total Cost**: The total amount invested (Quantity * Purchase Price).

8. **Market Value**: The current value of your investment (Quantity * Current Price).

9. **Unrealized Gain/Loss**: The difference between the market value and the total cost.

10. **% of Portfolio**: The percentage of each investment relative to the total portfolio value.

Step 3: Input Your Data

Enter the details for each investment in your portfolio. This process may require some research, especially for the current prices of your investments.

Step 4: Calculate Totals and Performance Metrics

Use spreadsheet formulas to calculate the Total Cost, Market Value, Unrealized Gain/Loss, and % of Portfolio for each investment. Also, calculate the overall performance of your portfolio.

Step 5: Regular Updates

Update the "Current Price" regularly to reflect the latest market conditions. This will automatically update the rest of your calculations, giving you an up-to-date view of your portfolio.

Example Spreadsheet Layout

Here is a simplified layout for an Investment Portfolio Tracker:

Investment Name	Category	Purchase Date	Quantity	Purchase Price	Current Price	Total Cost	Market Value	Unrealized Gain/Loss	% of Portfolio
XYZ Corp	Stocks	2024-01-10	100	$50	$55	$5,000	$5,500	$500	25%
ABC Mutual Fund	Mutual Funds	2023-07-15	200	$10	$12	$2,000	$2,400	$400	10%
Total						$7,000	$7,900	$900	100%

Investment Portfolio Tracker

Spreadsheet Formulas

- **Total Cost**: =C4*D4 for each row.

- **Market Value**: =E4*D4 for each row.

- **Unrealized Gain/Loss**: =G4-F4 for each row.

- **% of Portfolio**: =H4/SUM(H:H) for each investment, where **H:H** represents the entire Market Value column.

An Investment Portfolio Tracker spreadsheet is an invaluable tool for any investor seeking to stay informed about their investments' performance. By providing a clear overview of each investment's performance and the portfolio's overall health, it empowers investors to make strategic decisions, rebalance as necessary, and ultimately work towards their financial goals with greater precision and confidence. Regular maintenance and updates of the tracker are essential to ensure it accurately reflects the current state of your investments.

Insurance Policy Organizer

An Insurance Policy Organizer is a practical tool designed to keep track of all your insurance policies in one place, ensuring you have easy access to important information whenever needed. This can include health, auto, home, life, and any other insurance policies you might hold. By using a spreadsheet as your organizer, you can manage policy details, coverage limits, premiums, renewal dates, and contact information for each policy. This centralized approach simplifies the management of your insurance documents and helps ensure you're adequately covered across all areas of your life.

How to Create an Insurance Policy Organizer in a Spreadsheet

Step 1: List Your Policies

Begin by listing all the insurance policies you have. This could range from personal policies like health and life insurance to property-related ones such as home and auto insurance.

Step 2: Setup Your Spreadsheet

Open your preferred spreadsheet software and create a new document. Set up your spreadsheet with the following columns to capture essential information about each policy:

1. **Policy Type**: The type of insurance (e.g., Health, Auto, Home).

2. **Provider**: The insurance company or provider.

3. **Policy Number**: The unique identifier for your policy.

4. **Coverage Start Date**: When the coverage begins.

5. **Renewal Date**: When the policy is up for renewal.

6. **Premium**: The cost of the policy, indicating whether it's paid monthly, quarterly, or annually.

7. **Coverage Limits**: The maximum amount the policy will pay out.

8. **Deductible**: The amount you pay out of pocket before insurance kicks in.

9. **Contact Information**: Phone number and email address for claims or inquiries.

10. **Notes**: Any additional information relevant to the policy or coverage.

Step 3: Input Your Data

Fill in the spreadsheet with details for each of your insurance policies. This step may involve gathering documents or accessing information online from your insurance providers.

Step 4: Highlight Key Dates

Consider using conditional formatting to highlight renewal dates or coverage start dates that are approaching. This visual cue can help ensure you don't miss any important deadlines, such as renewals or payment due dates.

Step 5: Secure Your Data

Since this spreadsheet contains sensitive information, make sure to store it securely. Use password protection for the file, and consider backing it up in a secure location.

Example Spreadsheet Layout

Here's a simplified layout for an Insurance Policy Organizer:

Policy Type	Provider	Policy Number	Coverage Start Date	Renewal Date	Premium	Coverage Limits	Deductible	Contact Information	Notes
Auto	SuperInsure	123456789	2024-01-01	2024-12-31	$1,200/yr	$250,000	$500	555-1234	Full coverage
Home	HouseSafe	987654321	2024-01-15	2024-12-31	$800/yr	$500,000	$1,000	555-5678	Flood included
Health	HealthCarePro	456789123	2024-01-01	2024-12-31	$300/mo	Varies	$750	555-9012	PPO Plan

Insurance Policy Organizer

An Insurance Policy Organizer spreadsheet is an efficient and organized way to manage your insurance policies. It not only helps in keeping track of important details and dates but also ensures that you have all the necessary information at your fingertips when you need to make a claim or review your coverage. Regularly updating and reviewing your insurance organizer can save you time and help you make informed decisions about your insurance needs.

Estate Planning Checklist

An Estate Planning Checklist is a comprehensive tool designed to guide individuals through the process of organizing their estate affairs. It encompasses a wide range of tasks and documents needed to ensure your assets are managed and distributed according to your wishes upon your passing. This checklist can include wills, trusts, powers of attorney, healthcare directives, and more. Using a spreadsheet to create an Estate Planning Checklist allows you to systematically organize and track the completion of these crucial components.

How to Create an Estate Planning Checklist in a Spreadsheet

Step 1: Identify Essential Documents and Tasks

Begin by listing all the essential documents and tasks that are commonly included in estate planning. This can vary depending on individual circumstances but generally includes items like creating a will, setting up trusts, designating beneficiaries, and more.

Step 2: Setup Your Spreadsheet

Open your preferred spreadsheet software and create a new document. Set up your spreadsheet with the following columns to capture and organize the necessary information:

1. **Task/Document**: The name of the task or document to be completed.

2. **Description**: A brief description of the task or document and its purpose.

3. **Status**: Current status of the task (e.g., Not Started, In Progress, Completed).

4. **Due Date**: The target completion date for the task.

5. **Responsible Party**: The person responsible for completing the task, if applicable.

6. **Notes**: Any additional notes, such as locations of documents, contact information for attorneys, or other relevant details.

Step 3: Populate the Checklist

Enter all the tasks and documents you've identified into the spreadsheet, along with their descriptions and current statuses. If you're just starting, many items will likely be marked as "Not Started."

Step 4: Update Regularly

As you progress with your estate planning, regularly update the spreadsheet to reflect the current status of each task. This will help keep you on track and ensure no critical components are overlooked.

Step 5: Share With Trusted Individuals

Consider sharing this document or its details with trusted family members, your executor, or attorney to ensure that others are aware of your plans and the location of important documents.

Example Spreadsheet Layout

Here's a simplified layout for an Estate Planning Checklist:

Task/Document	Description	Status	Due Date	Responsible Party	Notes
Will	Legal document outlining asset distribution	In Progress	2024-06-01	John Doe	Attorney: Jane Smith, 555-1234
Living Trust	Avoids probate by setting up a trust	Not Started	-	-	Consider for real estate
Healthcare Directive	Specifies medical care preferences	Completed	2024-03-15	John Doe	Document stored in safe deposit box
Power of Attorney	Authorizes someone to act on your behalf	Completed	2024-03-20	Jane Doe	Jane Doe has original document
Beneficiary Designations	Designate beneficiaries for accounts	In Progress	2024-05-01	John Doe	Check retirement accounts and insurance
Digital Assets	List of digital assets and how to access	Not Started	-	-	Include social media, online accounts
Letter of Intent	Personal letter to executor and beneficiaries	Not Started	-	-	Clarify wishes not detailed in the will

Estate Planning Checklist

An Estate Planning Checklist in a spreadsheet is an invaluable resource for organizing your estate. It helps ensure that all necessary tasks are identified, tracked, and completed in a timely manner. Regularly updating and reviewing your checklist can provide peace of mind knowing that your affairs are in order, and your wishes will be honored. Sharing this checklist with key individuals involved in your estate planning ensures that everyone is informed and can act according to your plans.

Appendix B: Comprehensive Resource Directory

Financial Assistance Websites

Navigating the world of financial assistance can be daunting, but several websites offer invaluable resources, advice, and tools to help individuals and families manage their finances, seek financial aid, and access various forms of support. Whether you're looking for government assistance, scholarships, emergency relief funds, or financial planning tools, these websites are essential starting points for securing financial help.

1. **Benefits.gov**
    - **Website**: http://www.benefits.gov

    - **Description**: Benefits.gov is the official benefits website of the U.S. government. It provides a comprehensive database of government assistance programs. Users can explore a broad range of services, including healthcare, food and nutrition, disaster relief, and more. The site's Benefit Finder tool helps individuals find programs they may be eligible for.

2. Consumer Financial Protection Bureau (CFPB)

- **Website**: http://www.consumerfinance.gov

- **Description**: The CFPB offers consumers protection against unfair, deceptive, or abusive practices and takes action against companies that break the law. Their website provides tools and resources for managing personal finances, understanding consumer rights, and filing complaints about financial products or services.

3. National Foundation for Credit Counseling (NFCC)

- **Website**: http://www.nfcc.org

- **Description**: The NFCC offers access to credit counseling services, debt management advice, and financial education to help individuals achieve financial stability. Their counselors can provide guidance on budgeting, managing debt, and making informed financial decisions.

4. Federal Student Aid (FSA)

- **Website**: http://www.studentaid.gov

- **Description**: This U.S. Department of Education's website is a one-stop shop for applying for federal student aid. It includes information on grants, loans, and work-study funds for college or career school. The site also offers tools for managing loans and resources for financial planning for education.

5. USA.gov

- **Website**: http://www.usa.gov

- **Description**: USA.gov provides a portal to all government services and information, including financial assistance programs. It links to resources for jobs and unemployment, government benefits, housing help, and tax assistance, among others.

6. Feeding America

- **Website**: http://www.feedingamerica.org

- **Description**: Feeding America is a nationwide network of food banks that provides food assistance to millions of people in the United States. Their website can help individuals find local food banks and learn about food assistance programs.

7. The Simple Dollar

- **Website**: http://www.thesimpledollar.com

- **Description**: The Simple Dollar offers personal finance advice, tools, and reviews on financial products. It's a resource for learning about budgeting, saving money, paying off debt, and finding the best financial products to meet individual needs.

These websites are valuable resources for anyone seeking financial assistance or looking to improve their financial literacy. Whether you're dealing with debt, seeking help with education costs, or needing immediate financial support, these sites offer a starting point to find the help you need. Always ensure to visit the official and secure websites for accurate and up-to-date information.

Budgeting and Personal Finance Apps

Budgeting and personal finance apps have revolutionized the way individuals manage their money, offering tools to track spending, save money, invest, and plan for the future all from the convenience of a smartphone or computer. These apps vary in features, including budgeting tools, automatic categorization of expenses, investment tracking, and financial advice. Below is a list of popular budgeting and personal finance apps, along with their websites, to help you take control of your financial life.

1. Mint

- **Website**: https://www.mint.com

- **Features**: Mint is a widely used budgeting app that aggregates all your financial accounts in one place. It automatically categorizes transactions, tracks spending, provides budgeting suggestions, and monitors credit score.

2. You Need A Budget (YNAB)

- **Website**: https://www.youneedabudget.com

- **Features**: YNAB focuses on giving every dollar a job, offering a proactive approach to budgeting. It encourages users to plan for every expense and aims to help them break the paycheck-to-paycheck cycle and reduce debt.

3. Personal Capital

- **Website**: https://www.personalcapital.com

- **Features**: Personal Capital is best for investors who want to track their wealth and manage their finances in one place. It offers tools for budgeting, retirement planning, and investment checking, with a clear view of your asset allocation.

4. PocketGuard

- **Website**: https://www.pocketguard.com

- **Features**: PocketGuard simplifies budgeting by showing how much money is available for spending. It tracks income, bills, and recurring subscriptions, identifying opportunities to save.

5. Goodbudget

- **Website**: https://www.goodbudget.com

- **Features**: Goodbudget uses the envelope system for budgeting, allowing users to allocate money to different spending categories. It's great for sharing budgets with family members and works across multiple devices.

6. Acorns

- **Website**: https://www.acorns.com

- **Features**: Acorns is an investment app that rounds up your purchases to the nearest dollar and invests the spare change. It also offers retirement accounts and educational content to help grow your knowledge.

7. Stash

- **Website**: https://www.stash.com

- **Features**: Stash combines investing, banking, and budgeting in one app. It allows users to start investing with as little as $5, offering personalized guidance and a variety of investment options.

8. Simplifi by Quicken

- **Website**: https://www.simplifimoney.com

- **Features**: Simplifi by Quicken offers a customizable budgeting tool that tracks spending, subscriptions, and savings goals. It provides a financial planning workspace to manage your finances effectively.

These apps cater to a wide range of personal finance needs, from simple budgeting to comprehensive financial management. By exploring these options, you can find an app that aligns with your financial goals and preferences, helping you to manage your money more effectively and make informed financial decisions.

Government Assistance Program Links

Government assistance programs are designed to provide support to individuals and families in need, covering areas such as healthcare, food, housing, education, and employment. These programs aim to offer a safety net for those facing financial difficulties or other challenges. Below, you'll find a list of various government assistance program links, each leading to more information about the services offered and how to apply.

1. Supplemental Nutrition Assistance Program (SNAP)

- **Website**: https://www.fns.usda.gov/snap/supplemental-n utrition-assistance-program

- **Description**: SNAP offers nutrition assistance to millions of eligible, low-income individuals and families, providing electronic benefits that can be used like cash to purchase food.

2. Medicaid

- **Website**: https://www.medicaid.gov

- **Description**: Medicaid provides health coverage to millions of Americans, including eligible low-income adults, children, pregnant women, elderly adults, and people with disabilities.

3. Temporary Assistance for Needy Families (TANF)

- **Website**: https://www.acf.hhs.gov/ofa/programs/tanf

- **Description**: TANF provides financial assistance to help families with children achieve self-sufficiency. States receive block grants to design and operate programs that accomplish one of the purposes of the TANF program.

4. Federal Student Aid (FSA)

- **Website**: https://studentaid.gov

- **Description**: FSA provides grants, loans, and work-study funds for college or career school, offering more than $150 billion each year to help students pay for higher education.

5. Women, Infants, and Children (WIC)

- **Website**: https://www.fns.usda.gov/wic

- **Description**: WIC provides federal grants to states for supplemental foods, health care referrals, and nutrition education for low-income pregnant, breastfeeding, and non-breastfeeding postpartum women, and to infants and children up to age five who are found to be at nutritional risk.

6. Housing Choice Voucher Program (Section 8)

- **Website**: https://www.hud.gov/program_offices/public_indian_housing/programs/hcv

- **Description**: The Housing Choice Voucher program assists very low-income families, the elderly, and the disabled to afford decent, safe, and sanitary housing in the private market.

7. Low Income Home Energy Assistance Program (LIHEAP)

- **Website**: https://www.acf.hhs.gov/ocs/programs/liheap

- **Description**: LIHEAP helps keep families safe and healthy through initiatives that assist families with energy costs, providing federally funded assistance in managing costs associated with home energy bills, energy crises, and weatherization and energy-related minor home repairs.

8. Unemployment Insurance (UI)

- **Website**: https://www.dol.gov/general/topic/unemployment-insurance

- **Description**: Unemployment Insurance provides unemployment benefits to eligible workers who are unemployed through no fault of their own and meet other eligibility requirements of state law.

These websites are valuable resources for those seeking information on government assistance programs. They offer guidance on eligibility, application processes, and how to receive benefits, providing essential support to individuals and families in need.

Non-Profit Financial Education and Counseling Services

Non-profit financial education and counseling services play a crucial role in helping individuals and families manage their finances, reduce debt, and plan for the future. These organizations offer a range of services, including budget counseling, debt management plans, financial literacy workshops, and more, often at low or no cost. Below are several reputable non-profit organizations dedicated to financial education and counseling, along with their websites.

1. National Foundation for Credit Counseling (NFCC)

- **Website**: https://www.nfcc.org

- **Description**: The NFCC offers a wide range of financial counseling services, including credit and debt counseling, bankruptcy counseling, student loan debt counseling, and housing counseling. Their certified counselors provide guidance tailored to your unique financial situation.

2. Credit.org

- **Website**: https://www.credit.org

- **Description**: Credit.org provides financial education and counseling services aimed at helping individuals improve their financial literacy, manage their debts, and plan for their financial future. They offer services like debt management plans, financial workshops, and homebuyer education courses.

3. American Consumer Credit Counseling (ACCC)

- **Website**: https://www.consumercredit.com

- **Description**: ACCC offers credit counseling, debt management services, and financial education to consumers nationwide. Their goal is to help individuals achieve financial stability and understanding of financial literacy concepts.

4. Money Management International (MMI)

- **Website**: https://www.moneymanagement.org

- **Description**: MMI provides a full range of financial counseling services, including debt and budget counseling, debt management plans, student loan counseling, foreclosure prevention, and reverse mortgage counseling. They aim to improve lives through financial education.

5. GreenPath Financial Wellness

- **Website**: https://www.greenpath.com

- **Description**: GreenPath offers consumer credit counseling, debt management services, and financial education tools. They specialize in helping individuals and families work through financial challenges and achieve financial wellness.

6. Consumer Credit Counseling Service of San Francisco (CCCSSF)

- **Website**: https://www.cccssf.org

- **Description**: CCCSSF provides confidential financial counseling, debt management services, and financial education workshops to consumers. They focus on promoting financial literacy and helping people manage their money more effectively.

7. InCharge Debt Solutions

- **Website**: https://www.incharge.org

- **Description**: InCharge Debt Solutions offers credit counseling and debt management plans as well as financial education resources. They are committed to helping individuals achieve financial independence and reduce their debt.

8. Clarifi

- **Website**: https://www.clarifi.org

- **Description**: Clarifi offers personalized financial counseling, debt management, and housing counseling services. They also provide financial literacy workshops and educational resources to empower individuals to make informed financial decisions.

These non-profit organizations are dedicated to improving financial literacy and providing the tools and counseling necessary to navigate financial challenges. By accessing these resources, individuals can gain the knowledge and support needed to achieve financial stability and wellness.

Online Marketplaces and Gig Platforms

Online marketplaces and gig platforms have significantly transformed the way people buy, sell, and offer services across the globe. These platforms provide vast opportunities for freelancers, entrepreneurs, and businesses to reach a wider audience, while also offering consumers access to a diverse range of products and services. Whether you're looking to start a side hustle, grow your business, or find unique items, these websites are pivotal in connecting people and facilitating transactions.

Online Marketplaces

1. **Etsy**

   ○ **Website:** https://www.etsy.com

   ○ **Description:** Etsy is renowned for handmade, vintage items, and craft supplies. It's the go-to platform for artists, crafters, and collectors.

2. **eBay**

   ○ **Website:** https://www.ebay.com

   ○ **Description:** eBay offers a wide range of goods, from new and used products to rare and unique items, through both auction-style and direct sales.

3. **Amazon Marketplace**

   ○ **Website:** https://www.amazon.com

   ○ **Description:** Amazon Marketplace enables third-party sellers to sell new or used products on a fixed-price online marketplace alongside Amazon's regular offerings.

Gig Economy Platforms

1. **Upwork**

   ○ **Website:** https://www.upwork.com

   ○ **Description:** Upwork connects freelancers with businesses for a wide range of services, including writing, graphic design, web development, and marketing.

2. Fiverr

- ○ **Website**: https://www.fiverr.com

- ○ **Description**: Fiverr offers a platform for freelancers to offer services to customers worldwide, focusing on creative and digital services starting at $5.

3. TaskRabbit

- ○ **Website**: https://www.taskrabbit.com

- ○ **Description**: TaskRabbit connects individuals with local freelancers to help with everyday tasks such as cleaning, moving, delivery, and handyman work.

Specialized Platforms

1. Turo

- ○ **Website**: https://www.turo.com

- ○ **Description**: Turo is a car-sharing marketplace where individuals can rent out their vehicles to others, offering an alternative to traditional car rental services.

2. Airbnb

- ○ **Website**: https://www.airbnb.com

- ○ **Description**: Airbnb allows people to rent out their properties or spare rooms to guests, providing a unique and often more affordable alternative to hotels.

3. **Etsy**

- ○ **Website**: https://www.etsy.com

- ○ **Description**: Etsy is renowned for handmade, vintage items, and craft supplies. It's the go-to platform for artists, crafters, and collectors.

These online marketplaces and gig platforms offer flexible opportunities for earning income and accessing a global network of buyers and services. Whether you're an entrepreneur looking to expand, a freelancer seeking new projects, or a consumer in search of unique products and services, these platforms provide the tools and reach necessary to meet your needs.

Tax Assistance Resources

Navigating the complexities of tax laws and filing tax returns can be daunting for many individuals and businesses. Fortunately, there are numerous resources available to help with tax preparation, understanding tax laws, and even resolving tax issues. Below is a list of tax assistance resources, ranging from official government sites to non-profit organizations that offer free or low-cost tax help.

1. **Internal Revenue Service (IRS)**
   - Website: https://www.irs.gov

   - **Description**: The IRS website is the primary resource for federal tax information in the United States. It offers a wealth of information on tax laws, policies, and guidelines. Taxpayers can find forms, instructions, and tools for filing their taxes, including the Free File program for those who qualify.

2. Volunteer Income Tax Assistance (VITA)

- **Website**: https://www.irs.gov/individuals/free-tax-return
  -preparation-for-qualifying-taxpayers

- **Description**: The VITA program offers free tax help to
  people who generally make $57,000 or less, persons with
  disabilities, and limited English-speaking taxpayers who need
  assistance in preparing their own tax returns.

3. Tax Counseling for the Elderly (TCE)

- **Website**: https://www.irs.gov/individuals/tax-counseling
  -for-the-elderly

- **Description**: The TCE program offers free tax help for all
  taxpayers, particularly those who are 60 years of age and
  older, specializing in questions about pensions and retire-
  ment-related issues unique to seniors.

4. National Association of Tax Professionals (NATP)

- **Website**: https://www.natptax.com

- **Description**: The NATP is a professional association that
  provides tax professionals with education and resources.
  While it primarily serves tax professionals, taxpayers can use
  the site to find a tax preparer in their area.

5. Tax Foundation

- **Website**: https://www.taxfoundation.org

- **Description**: The Tax Foundation is a think tank that provides in-depth research and analysis on tax policies. Their

website offers resources and information that can help tax-payers understand complex tax issues and the broader implications of tax policies.

6. AARP Foundation Tax-Aide

- **Website**: https://www.aarp.org/money/taxes/aarp_taxaide

- **Description**: AARP Foundation Tax-Aide offers free tax preparation help to anyone, with a special focus on taxpayers who are 50 or older or who have low to moderate income. Tax-Aide volunteers are trained and IRS-certified.

7. Taxpayer Advocate Service (TAS)

- **Website**: https://www.taxpayeradvocate.irs.gov

- **Description**: TAS is an independent organization within the IRS that helps taxpayers resolve problems with the IRS and recommends changes to prevent future problems.

8. TurboTax Free File

- **Website**: https://turbotax.intuit.com/taxfreedom

- **Description**: TurboTax offers a Free File program for tax-payers with an adjusted gross income (AGI) of $39,000 or less, or those who qualify for the Earned Income Tax Credit (EITC). This online tool guides users through the tax filing process at no cost.

9. H&R Block Free File

- **Website**: https://www.hrblock.com/online-tax-filing/free-online-tax-filing

- **Description**: H&R Block provides a Free File option for taxpayers with an AGI of $72,000 or less. The program offers free federal and state tax filing with guidance to help taxpayers maximize their refunds.

These resources offer a variety of services to assist with tax preparation, filing, and questions, ensuring that taxpayers can access the help they need to navigate tax season successfully.

Community Resource Directories

Community Resource Directories are invaluable tools that compile and provide access to a wide range of local services, including healthcare, food assistance, housing support, educational programs, and legal aid. These directories are designed to help individuals and families find the assistance they need within their community. Below is a list of websites that offer comprehensive community resource directories across various regions and services.

1. United Way 211

- **Website**: https://www.211.org

- **Description**: United Way 211 provides free and confidential information and referral services for help with food, housing, employment, health care, counseling, and more. By dialing 211, individuals can connect with a wide range of services in their local community.

2. Aunt Bertha

- **Website**: https://www.auntbertha.com

- **Description**: Aunt Bertha offers an easy-to-use online platform for finding free and reduced-cost services like medical care, food, job training, and more. Users can search by zip code for services in their area.

3. FindHelp.org

- **Website**: https://www.findhelp.org

- **Description**: FindHelp.org, powered by Aunt Bertha, allows individuals to search for free or reduced-cost services like medical care, food, housing, and more, based on their location.

4. Community Resource Directory (CRD)

- **Website**: Varies by location; many local governments and nonprofit organizations host their own CRD websites. A quick search for "Community Resource Directory" followed by your city or county name can lead to a local directory.

5. Idealist

- **Website**: https://www.idealist.org

- **Description**: Idealist connects millions of idealists – people who want to do good – with opportunities for action and collaboration all over the world, including volunteer opportunities, nonprofit jobs, internships, and organizations working on various social issues.

6. HealthFinder.gov

- **Website**: https://healthfinder.gov

- **Description**: HealthFinder.gov provides information on health services, preventive measures, and various health-related topics. It's a resource offered by the U.S. Department of Health and Human Services.

7. Legal Services Corporation (LSC)

- **Website**: https://www.lsc.gov

- **Description**: LSC promotes equal access to justice in the United States by providing funding to legal aid organizations through the country to assist low-income individuals in obtaining legal representation.

8. Child Care Aware

- **Website**: https://www.childcareaware.org

- **Description**: Child Care Aware is a national network of Child Care Resource and Referral agencies (CCR&Rs) dedicated to providing news, resources, and assistance in finding quality child care and child care financial assistance.

9. Feeding America

- **Website**: https://www.feedingamerica.org

- **Description**: Feeding America is a nationwide network of more than 200 food banks that leads the fight against hunger in the United States. The website offers a food bank locator to help individuals find local food assistance programs.

10. Habitat for Humanity

- **Website**: https://www.habitat.org

- **Description**: Habitat for Humanity helps families build and improve places to call home. They believe affordable housing plays a critical role in strong and stable communities. The website provides information on their programs and how to get involved or seek assistance.

These community resource directories and platforms serve as a starting point for individuals seeking assistance, aiming to connect them with local services and support systems. Whether you're in need of immediate assistance or looking to volunteer and give back to your community, these resources can guide you in the right direction.

Financial Product Comparison Sites

Financial Product Comparison Sites are invaluable tools that help consumers make informed decisions by comparing a wide range of financial products and services, including credit cards, loans, savings accounts, insurance policies, and investment platforms. These websites offer detailed analyses, user reviews, and the ability to compare features and rates across multiple providers. Here's a list of prominent financial product comparison sites, each offering a unique set of tools and information to guide your financial decisions.

1. **NerdWallet**

   - **Website**: https://www.nerdwallet.com

   - **Description**: NerdWallet provides comparisons for various financial products, including credit cards, loans, insurance, investments, and banking. Their tools and advice are designed to help you understand your options and make the best choices for your financial situation.

2. **Bankrate**
   - **Website**: https://www.bankrate.com

   - **Description**: Bankrate offers detailed comparisons and reviews of mortgage rates, refinance rates, CDs, credit cards, auto loans, and more. They also provide calculators and financial advice to help users plan their finances.

3. Credit Karma

- **Website**: https://www.creditkarma.com

- **Description**: Credit Karma specializes in providing free credit scores and reports, along with comparisons for credit cards, loans, and auto insurance. They offer personalized recommendations based on your credit profile.

4. Compare The Market

- **Website**: https://www.comparethemarket.com

- **Description**: Based in the UK, Compare The Market allows users to compare prices and features of various insurance products, energy providers, financial services, and broadband packages.

5. MoneySuperMarket

- **Website**: https://www.moneysupermarket.com

- **Description**: MoneySuperMarket is a UK-based service offering comparisons for a wide range of financial products, including insurance, banking, energy, and broadband. They aim to provide users with the tools to find the best deals.

6. Finder

- **Website**: https://www.finder.com

- **Description**: Finder offers comparisons for credit cards, mortgages, savings accounts, insurance products, and personal loans. They provide guides and calculators to help users make informed financial decisions.

7. GoCompare

- **Website**: https://www.gocompare.com

- **Description**: GoCompare, another UK-based site, allows users to compare costs and features of insurance policies, financial products, and energy services, with a focus on finding the best deals and saving money.

8. The Zebra

- **Website**: https://www.thezebra.com

- **Description**: The Zebra is an insurance comparison site that provides quotes from over 200 providers for auto and home insurance, making it easier to find the best rates and coverage.

9. Policygenius

- **Website**: https://www.policygenius.com

- **Description**: Policygenius helps users compare and buy insurance online, including life, home, auto, and disability insurance. They provide unbiased advice and handle the application process.

10. ValuePenguin

- **Website**: https://www.valuepenguin.com

- **Description**: ValuePenguin focuses on providing in-depth analysis and comparison of financial products, particularly insurance, credit cards, and loans. They aim to simplify financial decisions through research and data.

These websites are designed to demystify the process of choosing financial products, offering a platform where consumers can easily compare options based on their needs and financial situations. Whether you're looking for the best insurance policy, the lowest mortgage rates, or the most rewarding credit cards, these comparison sites can provide valuable insights and help you make more informed financial decisions.

Emergency Fund and Investment Tools

Emergency funds and investment tools are essential components of a well-rounded financial plan, offering security in times of unexpected expenses and opportunities to grow wealth over the long term. Here's an overview of online resources and tools that can help you build an emergency fund, choose investment platforms, and manage your investments effectively.

Emergency Fund Tools

Creating and managing an emergency fund is crucial for financial security, helping you cover unexpected expenses without dipping into long-term savings or retirement accounts.

1. YNAB (You Need A Budget)

- Website: https://www.youneedabudget.com

- Description: YNAB focuses on budgeting and offers features to help you allocate funds for an emergency savings category, ensuring you're prepared for unexpected expenses.

2. Mint

- Website: https://www.mint.com

- Description: Mint is a popular personal finance app

that allows you to track your spending, create budgets, and set savings goals, which can include your emergency fund.

3. Ally Online Savings Account

○ Website: https://www.ally.com/bank/online-savings-account/

○ Description: Ally's high-yield savings account offers a competitive interest rate, making it a good place to store your emergency fund while earning interest.

Investment Tools

Investment tools can help you manage your portfolio, research investment options, and make informed decisions to grow your wealth.

1. Robinhood

○ Website: https://www.robinhood.com

○ Description: Robinhood offers commission-free trading of stocks, ETFs, and cryptocurrencies, catering to beginners and those looking for a straightforward investment platform.

2. Betterment

○ Website: https://www.betterment.com

○ Description: Betterment is a robo-advisor that provides automated portfolio management based on your goals and risk tolerance, including options for emergency fund savings within a low-risk investment strategy.

3. **Personal Capital**

- ◦ Website: https://www.personalcapital.com

- ◦ Description: Personal Capital offers wealth management services and free financial tools for tracking investments, net worth, and planning for retirement, making it suitable for more comprehensive financial planning.

4. **Vanguard**

- ◦ Website: https://www.vanguard.com

- ◦ Description: Vanguard is known for its low-cost index funds and ETFs, making it a good choice for long-term investors looking to build a diversified portfolio.

5. **Fidelity**

- ◦ Website: https://www.fidelity.com

- ◦ Description: Fidelity offers a wide range of investment options, including stocks, bonds, ETFs, and mutual funds, along with extensive research tools and resources for investors.

6. **Acorns**

- ◦ Website: https://www.acorns.com

- ◦ Description: Acorns rounds up your everyday purchases to the nearest dollar and invests the spare change, making it an easy way to start investing with small amounts of money.

7. **Morningstar**

- ○ Website: https://www.morningstar.com

- ○ Description: Morningstar is a leading provider of independent investment research, offering in-depth analysis and ratings of stocks, mutual funds, and ETFs to help investors make informed decisions.

These tools and resources can help you establish a solid financial foundation, whether you're building an emergency fund or looking to invest. Remember, it's important to research and choose the options that best fit your financial situation and goals.

Appendix C: Glossary of Financial Terms

This glossary provides definitions and explanations of common financial terms, offering a foundational understanding for anyone navigating the financial landscape. Whether you're managing personal finances, investing, or planning for the future, these terms are essential to know.

Asset

An asset is any resource owned by an individual or entity that has economic value and can provide future benefits. Assets can be tangible, such as real estate and vehicles, or intangible, such as stocks, bonds, and intellectual property. The value of an asset can be used to meet debts, commitments, or legacies.

Liability

A liability refers to any financial debt or obligation that an individual or entity owes to another party. Liabilities can include loans, mortgages, accounts payable, and other types of financial obligations that require payment in the future. The management of liabilities is crucial for financial stability and solvency.

Net Worth

Net worth is the total value of all assets owned by an individual or entity minus the total value of all their liabilities. It represents the financial position at a specific point in time and is a key indicator of financial health. A positive net worth indicates that assets exceed liabilities, while a negative net worth means liabilities exceed assets.

Interest Rate

The interest rate is the percentage of a loan amount charged by the lender to the borrower for the use of assets. Interest rates are typically expressed as an annual percentage of the principal. They can influence consumer spending, investment decisions, and the overall economy.

APR (Annual Percentage Rate)

APR stands for Annual Percentage Rate. It represents the annualized cost of credit, including interest and other charges, expressed as a percentage. The APR provides consumers with a bottom-line number they can easily compare with rates from other lenders or credit products.

Credit Score

A credit score is a numerical expression based on an analysis of an individual's credit files, representing the creditworthiness of the individual. Lenders use credit scores to evaluate the probability that an individual will repay loans in a timely manner. Scores are based on credit report information from credit bureaus.

Deductible

In the context of insurance, a deductible is the amount paid out of pocket by the policyholder before an insurance provider will pay any expenses. A higher deductible generally results in lower premium costs but means higher out-of-pocket costs when claiming.

Diversification

Diversification is an investment strategy that involves spreading investments among various financial instruments, industries, and other categories to reduce exposure to any single asset or risk. The goal of diversification is to maximize returns by investing in different areas that would each react differently to the same event.

Liquid Asset

A liquid asset is any asset that can be quickly converted into cash without significantly affecting its value. Examples include cash, savings accounts, and stocks. Liquid assets are important for meeting immediate and short-term financial obligations.

Bankruptcy

Bankruptcy is a legal process through which individuals or businesses unable to repay their outstanding debts can seek relief from some or all of their liabilities. The bankruptcy process involves the evaluation of the debtor's assets and liabilities by a court to determine the best course of action for debt repayment or discharge.

www.ingramcontent.com/pod-product-compliance
Lightning Source LLC
Chambersburg PA
CBHW071038290526
45795CB00004B/1205